What People Are Saying about *Your Most Powerful Question*

"This book is truly inspired. John masterfully combines both psychology and spirituality, something sorely needed in today's society. By helping each person to encounter themselves in a new way, discovering the question that undergirds their unique life story, Dr. John Olesnavage succeeds in helping them also to encounter the living God who dwells within. I have been deeply edified by this book."

—**Fr. Jordan Berghouse**, priest of the Archdiocese of Milwaukee, Wisconsin

"If you read this book and are not changed or at least awed, you have only turned pages. We have to drill down beyond the superficial questions to the most powerful question that lies within. Every page sharpens our clarity and baits our curiosity to move forward on this journey of personal discovery. Read and happy digging."

—**Mary C. Carroll, SSSF**, DMin, Professor Emeritus, Sacred Heart Seminary and School of Theology, author of *Spiritual Jewels: Five Wisdom Women*

"I have walked with many young adults who are thirsting to know who God created them to be and what God is asking of them. Discovering one's powerful question is a tool that can help these young adults discover the answers to these critical life questions."

—**Fr. Dustin Larson**, Catholic Campus Minister, Northern Michigan University

"*Finding Your Most Powerful Question* is a God-given gift at our present time. Discovering God and your purpose in life is one of the many blessings from discovering your question. When you realize God's love in your life and journey, you uncover a world of new possibilities. When I found my most powerful question, my entire approach to ministry changed."

—**Mary Lestina**, Pastoral Associate and adjunct faculty for the Diaconate Program in the Archdiocese of Milwaukee.

"Finding my powerful question has helped me understand my unique role in God's plan. It has given me clarity, focus, and a stronger determination to live it out every day. I encourage anyone of any age and background to take this inner pilgrimage! I was introduced to the program while studying for an advanced degree in theology, and I am thrilled it is now available to everyone."

—**M. Misey**, Vice President of Institutional Advancement, Sacred Heart Seminary and School of Theology

"A worthy journey to self-awareness on a deep spiritual level, the powerful question is life changing, impacting daily practice by distilling every aspect to a single focus. Join the difference-making community by unearthing your powerful question."

—**Patty O'Neal**, MSW Medical Social Worker for Hospice, choir member at St. Joseph's Catholic Church, Perkins, Michigan

"I was introduced to the powerful question approach to discernment in 2017 when I began studying for a master's degree in systematic theology. As a cradle Catholic who spent many decades away from the faith, discovering my powerful question was a transformative experience. My question helps me focus and discern appropriate action on a daily basis, and to recognize God's presence everywhere and in everything."

—**Edell M. Schaefer**, MLIS, MST, St. Dominic Catholic Parish, Brookfield, Wisconsin

YOUR MOST **POWERFUL** QUESTION

FINDING PURPOSE
AND MEANING IN
GOD'S PLAN

JOHN OLESNAVAGE, PhD

theWORD among us® press

Published by The Word Among Us Press
7115 Guilford Drive, Suite 100
Frederick, Maryland 21704
wau.org

26 25 24 23 22   1 2 3 4 5

ISBN: 978-1-59325-604-3
eISBN: 978-1-59325-605-0

Cover design by Suzanne Earl

Made and printed in the United States of America

Library of Congress Control Number:
2022900458

Contents

Introduction

When I was fifteen years old, I spent a week with family friends who owned a vegetable farm. It was a backbreaking introduction to farm life. What stands out most, however, is an incident with their son, who was a couple years older than I.

We were in the barn one day, and he was showing me how he could turn himself into a ghost by throwing handfuls of a white powder into the air and letting it float down over himself like a shroud. This was the same white powder we had been spreading on cabbage plants that morning. The way he laughed gave me the impression that he often played ghost. He urged me to join in, but I declined. It wasn't like me to pass up mischief, but something didn't seem right. My guardian angel was working overtime that day.

Years later I learned that the young man developed dementia in his thirties and died in his forties. Rachel Carson's book *Silent Spring* was released in 1962, the year of that incident in the barn. The author asked why we were exposing ourselves to harmful chemicals in order to grow more vegetables. Her question came too late to save my friend's life, but it set in motion a movement that spared the rest of us from exposure to the pesticide DDT.[1]

Warning us of impending disaster is just one example of the impact powerful questions can have on our lives. Not all questions are powerful, but most are practical. We use them to ask for permission, favors, and direction. We also use them to cross-examine suspected wrongdoers in order to determine innocence or guilt. Parents are especially adept at asking their children questions that can cut through the claim that "it wasn't me."

There are personal questions, professional questions, and scientific questions, to name but three types. And some questions sound personal in one context but not in another. The same question asked in a job interview, for example, can mean something entirely different when asked on a first date.

Essentially, most questions are simple requests for information. But this book is about a different kind of question, a life-changing question specific to each one of us. I call it the Most Powerful Question—because it is. As we will see, a question takes on the mantle of most powerful and animating when it originates in the themes and the narrative of our life.

When we discover our most powerful question, it leads to a new awareness of our truth, our purpose, and our place in God's plan. Pursuing an answer to this life-changing question moves us past self-limiting scripts we may have grown up with and directs us to what we desire most. It's the intentional way to discover our purpose and our place in God's plan.

A most powerful question isn't something we can conjure up, as if we're choosing the right answer by the process of elimination. Rather it's something we discover—because it is already there, embedded in our life story. As a discernment tool, our most powerful question involves a conscious effort to know what is authentic, unique, and special about ourselves.

Potential and Purpose

We can make list after list of our attributes, talents, and gifts while missing our real potential. That happens because potential without purpose always falls short. For example, we all have the potential to win the lottery if we buy a lottery ticket. Winning a million dollars in the lottery, however, doesn't ensure happiness, especially if we use our windfall without a sense of greater purpose, solely for our own gratification. Follow-up studies of lottery winners confirm the fact that many consider their lives ruined as a result of winning.

I spent years in search of some sort of completeness, some purpose, that felt big enough and compelling enough to engage me fully. I climbed a number of career ladders, but bigger paychecks and bigger job titles didn't fulfill my longing to make a significant difference. It seemed the harder I worked, the more "making a difference" seemed to move away. By the time I turned forty, I had pretty much accepted the idea that I was a dreamer who would never be satisfied. Ironically, what stopped my dreaming and gave me the purpose-filled life I longed for was not an answer but a question.

A single powerful question became my source of energy, focus, and direction. That question brought an awareness of what is essential and authentic in myself. Unraveling its mysteries has led me to discover who I am, who God is, and what hurdles in life I must clear.

I want this same satisfaction for you. Climbing ladders and chasing dreams are just that—climbing and chasing— if we haven't found the single powerful question that gives us a path to purpose.

Four Starting Points

Finding your most powerful question works for anyone who wants a purpose-filled life, no matter your starting point. With that said, in the years of helping others find their most powerful question, I have identified four typical starting points: (1) Some start because they're ready to find what is true and gifted about themselves. (2) Others start because they feel drawn to achieve or create something unique and special. (3) A starting point for some is the desire to make a difference, contribute to the greater good, and leave a legacy. (4) Still others start because they want to discern what God wants them to do next.

These four starting points are likely to correspond to a person's stage of development. Young people naturally focus on relationships, visualizing goals, and building a future. Middle-aged adults typically focus on resources and family responsibilities. Mature adults are likely to think in terms of leaving a legacy. No matter the age, adults who feel fairly settled and fulfilled typically want to know what God wants of them next.

What all four starting points have in common is the sense of being called to something greater. For the Christian, there is added the belief that God has a special role for them in his plan. This book is for those who are willing to discover their most powerful question and the passionate life God intends for them.

?

CHAPTER ONE

Powerful Questions and Spiritual Growth

As a kid in Catholic elementary school, I often heard teachers tell us we were called to be saints. In grade school, I found that message inspiring, and I even made brief attempts to imitate St. John Vianney and St. Francis of Assisi. My efforts to fast and abstain from food usually lasted about three hours, and never past lunchtime.

As I grew older, I found the idea of being a saint somewhat troubling. The saints I had read about were pretty out there. They ate locusts, they endured torture, they lived as outcasts and beggars. They chose to hang out with lepers, and they heard voices. In many stories in Butler's *Lives of the Saints,* there is ample evidence of behavior that would qualify as strange, if not abnormal. The more I learned about saints, the less attracted I was to sainthood.

Although I gave up on trying to act like a saint by my sophomore year in high school, I continued to believe that we are all called to a special role in God's plan. I could see that idea play out not only in the lives of canonized saints but also in the bigger-than-life men and women who changed entire industries and caused momentous social change. On the industrial, scientific, and entertainment side, we have Walt Disney, Madame Curie, Albert Einstein, and Thomas Edison. On the social justice side, we have Dr. Martin Luther King, Jr., Cesar Chavez, and Dorothy Day, to name just a few. One person can move mountains!

Such people are so passionate and so consumed by their visions that they become seemingly indifferent to public opinion. These visionaries tap into something similar to the passion and purpose that saints possess. All of these individuals, especially Cesar Chavez and Dorothy Day, helped me see the possibilities in my own life.

My awareness of my most powerful question began in 1995, when I was what I would describe as a lukewarm Catholic. I had worked for over twenty years in various social work and human service positions and had many questions about many things, especially the best ways to serve those in need. I returned to graduate school looking for answers but instead found a single question embedded in my life story. That question led me to a new understanding of fulfillment and a deeper relationship with Jesus Christ.

It brought about a renewed appreciation for my Catholic faith and its importance in my life. Now my mission, my ministry, is to help others find the most powerful question in their life story.

Finding a powerful question is finding the path to truth and God, the author of all truth. Jesus called the apostle Andrew not with a command or suggestion but rather with a life-changing question, "What are you looking for?" (John 1:38). The apostles followed Jesus, and they formed the nucleus of the greatest spiritual renewal in human history.

That same question, "What are you looking for?" forms the nucleus of our most powerful question. It continues to call us today.

Powerful questions have always provided the spark for spiritual renewal. Four hundred years ago, a country priest by the name of Vincent de Paul told the story of a poor family and repeatedly asked, "What must be done?"[2] That question continues to be the driving force behind the Vincentian order and the charitable work carried out by the Society of St. Vincent de Paul around the world.

At the age of five, Thomas Aquinas asked, "What is God?" Years later that question was still churning in him as he wrote his *Summa Theologiae*. In that monumental work, St. Thomas provided an answer to that five-year-old's question and to many other questions. His pursuit of an answer to his powerful question became the underpinning of Catholic theology as we know it today. Thomas Aquinas is proof that a most powerful question will evolve as we do.

Jesus said, quite emphatically, "I am the vine, you are the branches" (John 15:5). Branches are not there just to look pretty or sway in the wind. Branches are there to produce leaves, flowers, fruit, and the seeds to generate more trees. Each of us "branches" has a specific calling that requires the talents and gifts we have been given. Pursuing that calling is pursuing passion, purpose, and God. That's the definition of "saint" I can and do embrace.

The Stories We Live

We are born into God's salvation story, a story of incarnation, death, and resurrection. At Baptism we are initiated into the life of the Church and become participants in Christ's life and mission. We have a role to play in the salvation story, and we become equipped, through the sacraments and our ongoing spiritual growth, to make a difference.

Human beings are hardwired to look for meaning and purpose. We Catholics believe that God supplies both. Our task is to determine what they are and do our best to fulfill them.

We tend to think of ourselves as a blend of family values, cultural influences, and personality traits. But we are much more. We are God's creation; we share God's DNA. We have a specific purpose, and the clue to that purpose is a powerful question embedded in our life story. This book is about finding that question and ultimately that purpose.

As adults, we take our story for granted, assuming that we know it pretty well or certainly well enough. We feel we have a sense of who and what we are. A powerful question can take us further, enabling us to explore our *why*. That why is embedded in one or more of the main themes of our life story.

A theme is a recurring idea or motif that runs through a story. There are themes that run through our lives as well, especially in the ways we interpret our experiences. For example, do we tend to interpret experiences negatively or positively? If we have a flat tire on the way to a much-anticipated gala event, we might consider it a random occurrence, or we might see it as the way things always go wrong when we have high expectations. The ways we respond to life's challenges and opportunities—the patterns we tend to follow—form part of the themes of our life.

Challenges can be as simple as getting up on time and as complex as choosing an end-of-life care plan for our parents. Opportunities can be as simple as trying out for the high school basketball team and as complicated as having two job offers in two different states at the same time. We react to these circumstances in different ways, but some ways of reacting become ingrained and repeat more often than others. These ways of acting, thinking, and feeling—both conscious and unconscious—form dominant themes. Our most powerful question is embedded in a dominant theme and usually points to an underlying intention or desire.

What do I mean by that? Simply put, there are underlying intentions involved in anything we avoid and in anything we seek. Underlying intentions run the gamut. Two of the most familiar are self-protection and striving for affirmation.

If we only trust those who first demonstrate that they are trustworthy, then we might typically operate from a stance of self-protection. And striving to achieve perfect grades in school might indicate a desire to get affirmation from parents who have high expectations.

Intentions are not always obvious, even to ourselves. That's especially true when the longing is for something indefinable but nevertheless palpable, a little like that never-satisfied feeling some of us experience.

Our most powerful question will represent something we truly do not know about a major theme in our life. It is more unconscious than conscious, and it touches at the core of who we are. A visceral reaction will always arrive with that question, to tell us it is exactly what we need to explore, understand, and embrace. Like the doctor's tap of a hammer on our knee, our cells react strongly to this moment of clarity and truth.

Why do we have such a strong reaction? Because the question ignites our passion, reveals our truth, and leads us to our place in God's plan.

Letting Your Question Emerge

Your most important question is embedded threadlike in the fabric of your life story from an early age. It emerges when something triggers it, much the way we suddenly notice—when shopping, for example—that music is playing in the background. Our question can also surface at times of crisis, when we run out of answers.

Monica was a corporate marketing manager who taught marketing at the college level. After a successful career, she retired in order to spend more time with her children. She went back to school to study theology when she was fifty-four. Her introductory studies included a course on finding her powerful question. When asked to reflect on her question and what it means to her, she shared the following:

She sat nervously in the large recliner wheelchair. I remember the blue plastic vinyl of the seal and the striped canvas seatbelt that kept her from falling out. The non-skid socks on her feet, the clothes too large over her bony frame, her wrinkled hands nervously fumbling. This shell used to be my mother, but her mind had abandoned her.

If you have sat with someone with dementia, you know that life can be very volatile. One moment can be filled with joy, the next sorrow or anger. There were sobs, laughs, groans. Perhaps the worst were the few moments of clarity when she understood her situation, but then the moment passed and she faded away again.

That's when I learned the incredible value of each and every moment. Giving her one moment of peace would be all I could try to do, one moment at a time, but for that moment, it was her entire world. I started to ask myself, "What love is needed in the moment?"

Flash forward several years to a hurting, anxious, and angry teenager yelling at me. Her face was red and tearstained, her body tense, her voice loud. Her passionate nature was a blessing at times but also took its toll at times. I looked at her and saw the hurting toddler locked away inside and wondered how I could help her feel more loved by the end of this conflict than she felt at that moment. I continued to ask, "What love is needed in the moment?"

When my oldest sister, Karen, passed away suddenly, I went to her daughter's home. Karen's children had gathered there with their young children. I knocked, the door opened, and it was dark inside. Sobbing hung in the air. You could feel the hurt, as if a strong, hot wind came out and hit me in the face. I crossed the threshold, and there was only one question I could ask myself: "What love is needed in the moment?"

I am so thankful to know my powerful question. I didn't know it was my powerful question back then, but it was there. Now I use it with intentionality. It guides which work I pursue and how I respond to situations, and it grounds me. If I stay true to living my powerful question, things are not always rosy, but they are clear. More often than not, I can allow love to heal a moment, and moment by moment, that is good enough for me.

"Good enough for me" is a humble statement from a humble person who is already making a difference, both as a leader in her parish and as an administrator in a major seminary. Monica recognized that the question that kept surfacing at those unsettling times, "What love is needed in the moment?" was in fact her powerful question and the lens through which she now looks at life.

The Impact of Questions

Can a single question change your life and impact the world? It may seem improbable, but dig a little. You will find that most extraordinary people—people like Albert

Einstein, Steve Jobs, and Rachel Carson—followed a single question that propelled them beyond the ordinary and into the history books.

Albert Einstein's question arrived when he was sixteen. He is reported to have said later in life that his question, "What would it be like to ride on a beam of light?"[3] followed him through all his discoveries.

Watching while his friend Steve Wozniak wired a computer in 1976, Steve Jobs asked out loud whether one computer might someday be able to talk with another computer directly.[4] Today that question is a no-brainer, but in 1976 it was borderline delusional (and visionary).

Rachel Carson's question about the use of DDT and other poisons on our crops brought a new level of awareness to consumers who would never have read a scientific journal. Her *Silent Spring* helped ignite a demand for healthy, poison-free food that most of us expect and even take for granted today.

Whether our question sounds scientific or grounded in personal meaning, it will lead us to the truth and the life we were born to live. Our lives present us with many choices, but the core values that lead us to salvation remain the same. The Ten Commandments have not changed; neither has the love God expressed by sending his Son to die for us on the cross.

How does having a most powerful question impact our faith journey? Simply put, it gives us a lens to examine our life and our relationship with God. In fact, adult spiritual growth only begins when we start asking what our faith means in terms of who and what we are. A powerful question propels spiritual growth because it helps us enter into our God-given purpose, where we can encounter the truth and deepen our relationship with the Lord.

Questions that help us develop a deeper relationship with God are those that emerge from our own life themes. God knows our powerful question; indeed, he had a hand in planting it in our life story. Asking God's help in finding it is more than appropriate.

?

CHAPTER TWO

Discovering
My Question

I was dissatisfied in my work and looking for answers in 1995 when I began my journey to my most powerful question. I returned to graduate school, enrolling in the Center for Humanistic Studies, now known as the Michigan School of Psychology. My first supervision session was with Dr. Clark Moustakas, cofounder of the school with Dr. Cereta Perry. The session proved to be a turning point in my life, the true beginning of what has since become my life's mission.

Anxious to glean all I could from our conversation, I started by asking Dr. Moustakas how he was able to accomplish everything he did, including writing numerous books and starting a graduate school that inspired many to pursue their dreams. He gave me a wry smile and said, "I just follow my question every day."

Confused, I asked what his question was, expecting to hear a deep philosophical answer with big words I would have to look up later. Instead I heard "What is loneliness?" I knew the title of one of his most popular books was *Loneliness*, but I did not realize that this existential question also motivated and drove his life.

To be honest, I wasn't much interested in loneliness, but as I listened to Dr. Moustakas that day, I felt I was hearing the recipe for a lifetime of fulfillment. And with no clue as to the spiritual journey I was embarking on, I immediately set out to find a question that would work as well for me as his did for him.

I began by researching the concept of questions. I repeatedly came across the Greek philosopher Socrates, who lived four centuries before Christ. It was Socrates who first elevated questions to a science. His method, the Socratic method, is the style of instruction in law schools today. It's a way of peeling back layers of rationalizing and defensive reasoning in search of truth, with questions such as "Do you think, or do you know?" "How do you know?"

Socrates was seventy-one and a decorated hero from the Peloponnesian War when he was charged with crimes against the city-state of Athens and condemned to death. Among other charges, he was accused of corrupting the youth of Athens by insisting that they ask questions of those in authority. He refused to stop teaching and instead accepted his death sentence. In his final day in court, he declared, "An unexamined life is one not worth living." The next day he drank the poison hemlock and died.

Where Are My Boundaries?

Socrates laid the foundation, and Dr. Moustakas supplied the inspiration, for my journey to discover my most powerful question. Then Dr. Cereta Perry brought my question home for me.

I met with Dr. Perry to present a case study involving a dysfunctional family. I thought my presentation went well, but when I finished, she responded with a penetrating look and dead silence for several uncomfortable moments. Finally she shot me a question that pierced through skin and bone: "Where are your boundaries?"

I froze, like a deer caught in the headlights. My what? Was this a rhetorical question, or was it serious criticism? Ordinarily I would have risen to the challenge and defended my assessment and my proposed plan. But Dr. Perry's tone of voice told me that this was not about the case I'd just presented. It wasn't a jab at my approach or a poke at my outlined strategy. Her pointed question was about *me*.

I stalled, searching her eyes for an escape route and seeing none. I wanted to cry out, "I don't think I know what having a boundary is!" but I thought it best not to share that reflection. When I could stall no longer, I asked if she thought "boundary" was something I should consider researching. Her reply was a terse "I think so."

I left Dr. Perry's office that afternoon with intense feelings pushing against each other in my chest, making breathing difficult. On the one hand, I felt exposed and vulnerable, and on the other hand, the way I was reacting told me that I had just been handed a question that had the power to change the course of my life.

But why did Dr. Perry's question challenge me? What did it trigger in me? "Boundary" was the chain-link fence my father put up to keep me and my siblings contained in our yard. It slowed us down for the time it took to climb over the top rail, ripping another pair of trousers.

"Boundary" was also the "don't even ask" look my father gave me when I approached him with certain requests. Knowing the answer was probably no, I wouldn't ask. At a young age, I learned to go after what I wanted through a "side door." On the plus side, this fostered the independent spirit I have to this day. On the negative side, it left me ignorant of how to seek guidance or negotiate support from those in authority.

As you can imagine, this played out in numerous detrimental ways, especially during my teen years. By the time I arrived at college, climbing over, under, and around boundaries was second nature. Not only did I cut corners, but I sought them out like some sort of Rambo with a combat knife clenched between his teeth.

This is why Dr. Perry's question hit me like a ton of bricks. It exposed an issue that was central to who I was and how I approached life. Apparently she saw this in me. I spent the days and weeks after our supervision session reflecting on what had occurred.

Eventually I realized that my disregard for boundaries was only part of the picture. The other part was not understanding what boundaries are or what value they have. I quickly realized that finding an answer to "Where are your boundaries?" was critical to discovering who and what I was as a person. It became and remains my most important question, guiding my work and propelling my personal and spiritual life.

I even wrote a book about boundaries—*Our Boundary* (Dog Ear, 2009)—that includes information about what it takes to repair stuck or torn boundaries. I am forever grateful to Dr. Perry for her challenge!

The Level beyond the Dream

A powerful question can grow out of and connect with a person's life story. This question can sound personal (like mine) or seemingly impersonal, like Einstein's question about riding on a beam of light. A powerful question may come like a thunderbolt or a warm breeze, but it is distinct and revealing enough to cause that visceral reaction I spoke of earlier. Our unique life stories and the narratives they produce give rise to the powerful questions that wait patiently to be discovered.

Passionate, committed individuals have asked powerful questions that transformed their lives. Read any biography of a person in the public eye, and you are likely to witness this process in the unfolding of their story. I've mentioned Albert Einstein; how about Harriet Tubman, Rosa Parks, and Johann Sebastian Bach? Each of their contributions can be traced to a powerful question in their life story. That question may not appear obvious at first, but dig a little, and you will find the one that led them to their break-throughs and legacies.

As my boundary question continued to awaken new levels of spiritual awareness in me, I began telling clients that there was a level above pursuing a dream. That level was finding and pursuing a single question that ignites passion and reveals purpose. What I didn't tell them, but what I was starting to understand, was that they would most surely meet God on that journey. Clients began asking how they might pursue their own discovery process, and I began leading classes focused on finding your most powerful question.

A ripple effect of the initial class emerged when one of the participants, Curt Hewitt, and I went mountain biking together. I loved mountain biking, but Curt was younger and in better shape, so it was no surprise to find him waiting for me at the top of a particularly steep hill. Partly to catch my breath and partly to slow him down, I started a conversation.

I shared that for years I had dreamed of starting a program to see what impact mountain biking could have for youth who were getting in trouble. I believed it would change their lives for the better. But that was a question that still needed an answer.

Curt agreed that it sounded like a good idea. I told him that while I'd thought about organizing such an effort, I wouldn't take it on alone. Without blinking an eye, Curt said, "I'll do it with you." That program, now called "Start the Cycle," was born in that question, "Could mountain biking turn troubled young lives around?"

That was 2013, and we spent the year building the program by trial and error. With the support of the juvenile court in Marquette County, a few volunteer mentors, and donated bikes, the program took off. In that first year, we helped sixteen young boys and girls prepare for and finish the Ore-to-Shore twenty-eight-mile mountain-bike race.

The participants' reward for finishing the race was two-fold. The first reward was the pride they felt for completing the race and hearing the cheers of families, probation officers, and friends at the finish line. The second reward was keeping the bikes and the riding gear: helmet, jersey, shorts, water pouch.

Our reward? Seeing their ear-to-ear grins as they crossed the finish line, knowing that they had achieved something that might change their lives. And yes, watching them complete the race was crossing another boundary for me. That boundary was the one created by those who said a program like this wouldn't work, that a twenty-eight-mile race would be too much for "this kind" of youngster.

Laura MacDonald, another participant in that initial powerful question class, kept the biking program rolling. "Start the Cycle" is now a nonprofit that works with thirty-five area youth per year and enlists the help of over twenty mentors and volunteers.

Laura's powerful question is "What is legacy?" She learned that leaving a legacy is a high-value gift, not only for herself but also for the community volunteers who help her train and mentor youth. One gentleman, a retired business owner, told her that he felt his mentoring effort was the most meaningful event in his life.

Laura is responding to her powerful question and building her legacy, one bike ride at a time. She's touching the lives not only of young people participating in the program but also of her dedicated crew of volunteers who trust her leadership and share her vision.

Following My Question

After offering classes on the most powerful question for a few years, I felt a growing need to bring this concept to a larger community. I envisioned an organization that would provide structure for such an undertaking. But I had a barrelful of self-doubt. Was I ready for such an undertaking?

On a beautiful late summer day in 2015, I was eating lunch while reading *Come Be My Light,* a book that not only chronicles Mother Teresa's powerful vocation but also reveals her struggle with a sense of God's absence—a "dark night"—that lasted nearly fifty years.[5] As I read, my thoughts strayed to the powerful question organization I dreamed of starting. Every few minutes, I would catch myself and refocus on reading. Mother Teresa describes her 1946 train ride to Darjeeling, India, when God instructed her to leave her comfortable convent and her work as a teacher and devote the rest of her life to serving the poorest of the poor in India's slums.

I read on, but all the while I felt a strong urge to start my venture. Meanwhile the start-up seemed impossible: I needed more money, more time, more network, and some sort of sign that this was the right move. Rereading the page about Mother Teresa's train ride for the third time, I finally felt something poking at my awareness. Comprehension arrived, and the words on the page finally registered.

Mother Teresa's call to action from God occurred on September 10, 1946. The date that day, as I was reading and eating my sandwich, was September 10, 2015. I had wanted a sign, and this was it. A very short time later, I gathered a group of initial supporters and established the nonprofit My Powerful Question Institute, Inc.

When we are following our powerful question and pursuing God's purpose for our life, we can expect divine intervention to occur as a matter of course. Ultimately, my most powerful question not only led me to establish the institute; it also, and foremost, led me to a deeper walk with God and my family and a life of service in helping others find their purpose.

?

CHAPTER THREE

Purpose Begins Here

Purpose brings the question that pries open reluctant eyelids each morning: "Is today the day that brings what I long for?" Our immediate wish may be for a promotion or a smile from an angry teenager, but that longing rubs up against a deeper question.

Purpose begins when all else falls away and we are left with only a single, compelling, powerful question. The truth we find there draws us to God's purpose.

The word "calling" is often used interchangeably with "purpose." Our calling can arrive like a whisper, as if carried on the wind, or it may arrive in a more disruptive manner, as Paul's did on his way to Damascus (see Acts

9:1-9). It may reach us through the words of a teacher or a friend or in a persistent longing for future achievement.

Ideally, our calling is apparent in our career or vocation, but a career is not the same thing as a calling. All too often, career is little more than the expedient path of least resistance. That is, a mother was a lawyer and pointed her son or daughter in that direction, or a father was an electrician and was able to get his son or daughter into the apprentice program.

We often ask young children, "What do you want to be when you grow up?" This is the first of many messages a child receives that career and identity are the same thing. As we mature, we discover that this is simply not true. But for some who are "married" to their work, this awareness may arrive too late.

We want our work to be rewarding and a source of pride, but it is only part of our identity. We are more than the sum of our parts. The job we are doing, and what we appear to be good at, may well serve our God-given purpose, our calling in life. But in connection with God's plan, purpose is always larger than career.

Thanks to longer life spans and a rapidly changing world, a new career paradigm has emerged, one that forces us to redefine what we call "career." The new paradigm includes a second (and sometimes third) occupation. Whether forced by job restructure, layoffs, financial need, or longer life spans, many of us between the ages of thirty and sixty seek work quite different from the one we prepared for in school. Sometimes we change course completely. I know a woman in her fifties who has three different master's degrees and has had three different careers: in engineering, physical therapy, and rabbinic studies.

These second (or third or fourth) careers are also opportunities to rediscover and resuscitate childhood dreams and the belief that all things are possible with God. Renewing that belief is made easier with the help of a powerful question, moving us past all the "shoulds" and "ought tos" that can block our progress. Reigniting a belief in God's omnipotence opens the door to conversion, a necessary step if we are to grow in our faith and find purpose.

"Conversion" generally refers to a change or to being changed, but the word has other shades of meaning. I once asked a priest for a definition of "conversion," and he replied: "Simple. It's the day you recognize that God is God, and you are not."

I repeat that definition to myself daily. It says it all. I consider career, and how we approach career, a good way to measure whether we recognize that "God is God, and we are not."

Finding the right next "career" requires an honest self-appraisal and some soul searching. We need to stop thinking career and start thinking fulfillment and God's purpose for our life. What difference are we called to make? What legacy does God want us to leave? We can try to find out through trial and error, but the more focused way is to find the powerful question in our life story.

Not every powerful question will sound spiritual, but they can all begin a spiritual journey. It's God's universe, and his purpose unfolds by bits and pieces as we find and begin to follow our powerful question. This journey is life changing for us, even as St. Paul's spiritual journey was for him. The benefits are beyond what we could imagine ahead of time.

Stepping into the Unknown

Because a powerful question links purpose to calling, it's especially valuable for endeavors that require creativity and artistic expression. Purpose is often taken for granted, overlooked, or assumed. Maya Lin, a design architect extraordinaire, built a career and a legacy by exploring purpose as have few others.

Maya was still an undergraduate student in 1981 when she entered and won the design competition for the Vietnam Veterans Memorial in Washington, DC. Her design, the Vietnam Veterans Wall, is considered as moving and lasting a memorial as any that exist. In her book *Boundaries,* she explains that she began the design process for the memorial by asking herself a single question, "What is the purpose of a war memorial at the close of the twentieth century?"[6]

Staying true to her creative process, which begins by exploring purpose, Maya Lin has gone on to design numerous other sculptures and land art projects, including the Civil Rights Memorial in Montgomery, Alabama, and the Women's Table at Yale University.

Maya Lin's design process reminds us that purpose is essential.

I wonder what would happen if we were to ask what purpose the Church serves in our lives here in the early years of the twenty-first century. I think the answer to that question could help determine future direction. And who else is going to answer that question but us?

I directed a lay ministers' retreat, where I met Patty, a devout and committed Catholic who is active in her parish. During one of the breaks, she pointed out a wooden mosaic on the wall behind the altar in the chapel. It consisted of hundreds of wood blocks cut to various shapes and sizes. She told me that she knew exactly which piece represented her and her place in the Church.

I was so impressed by Patty's conviction that I spent twenty minutes looking for the piece that looked like "me." I found it, and I must admit that it did feel good to see my place in the mosaic of the Catholic Church. That place supports and is supported by all the other pieces.

Purpose begins a journey, one in which I neither know nor control the outcome. On this journey, I live not only with the tension of forming my own path but also with the tension of being formed by it, one step at a time. It is the path Mother Teresa followed when she heard God telling her to leave her secure convent and move to the poorest part of Calcutta. It is the path of people everywhere who leave what might be comfortable and familiar, risking the unknown, in order to pursue the purpose and meaning to which God calls them.

?

CHAPTER FOUR

Moving Past Preconceived Notions

Consider the internet. Initially it was a novel way to communicate with a closed circuit of academic and business associates, then it expanded to include friends and relatives. It didn't take many years after that for it to replace—or at least greatly diminish—other forms of communication, such as handwritten letters and phone calls.

What role did powerful questions play in this technological advancement?

Earlier I offered the example of Steve Jobs' wondering if one day computers might be able to communicate directly with one another. In 1976 that question seemed to be from the realm of science fiction, and yet here we are. What do we think is beyond our imagination—unattainable and bigger than life—in our present situation?

Steve Jobs was able to see the question that would animate the rest of his life. We are all able to see our powerful question, but we have to look closely and patiently. We then need to give voice to what comes from the depths of our life story. Recognizing our most powerful question is the first step in leaving a legacy of our own.

Many of us walk through the smorgasbord of life and fill our plates with whatever is in front of us, without ever asking whether there are other choices. We settle for being fed. A powerful question doesn't just give us more food choices; it enables us to examine the entire eating experience and empowers us to make choices based on our resultant knowledge.

In the field of nutrition, that kind of questioning and awareness galvanized the vegan movement. In education, that kind of questioning and awareness spawned home-schooling and charter schools.

Ignite Your Passion

A powerful question is the match that ignites our passion and leads us to what we were born to do. Passion is giving 100 percent and being willing to risk failure, whether we are trying to find a cure for cancer, pitch a no-hitter, or bake the best apple pie. We see that passion in young children when they run full tilt into a parent's embrace. Those hugs can resuscitate and breathe life into a weary day.

Passion is not something we experience only in peak moments; it is life force. We adults might find our passion reduced to a barely flickering flame by the demands and pressures of life. Torches are not always easy to find, and some arrive in strange ways.

I told you about my passion for off-road cycling; needless to say, there is more to the story. At age forty-three, I fell into a depression in the aftermath of my eleven-year-old daughter Tami's death from a brain tumor. That was the obvious cause, but in truth I had already been in the throes of what is typically referred to as a midlife crisis.

I was working at a job I found unfulfilling. Even before Tami's death, my habit was to come home each night and disappear into my barn or my garden to destress. This worked to a degree, but a result was that I became less and less visible, even to myself. My family learned, for the most part, to carry on without me. As I self-isolated, I became stuck in an ever-deepening state of despair.

This depression went on for over a year, until I realized I had a decision to make. I could stay stuck in a cocktail of depression and grief, or I could choose life. I chose life, but then I had to face the fact that I had no idea what having a life meant.

Looking around for ways to jump-start my life, I turned to my brother Joe. He was an avid cyclist and health advocate. Initially the thought of getting on a bicycle in my mid-forties seemed rather childish, but I knew I had to start somewhere. I bought a used bike and started riding.

To say I was rusty is an understatement. However, I kept at it, and old feelings began to emerge. These were feelings I had felt at age nine or ten: wind in my face, going down hills that took my breath away. "Look, Ma, no hands!"

Cycling became my connection and my doorway to passion. I began bicycle touring, which led to off-road mountain biking, which led to races, which led to a trip across England, Scotland, and Wales. I learned that if I could climb steep hills on a bike, I could go back to school and pursue a PhD. And I am no longer invisible. My wife, children, and grandchildren now share my biking adventures and my passion, not only for two-wheel fun but for life.

My passion for bicycling was what brought me out of the midlife crisis, but it took my powerful question to understand that the biggest hills were still in front of me. It took many years to find my powerful question, to develop a way to help others find their powerful question, and to connect my question to my Catholic faith and my faith journey. I climb bigger and bigger hills as I feel the Holy Spirit moving in my life. Conquering a steep hill for the first time is a peak moment (excuse the pun), but nothing compares to the top of the hill, where God waits for us.

Be Motivated

"Motivation" stems from the Latin word *movere*, which means "to move." We are hardwired to move. Little children run and jump naturally, with seemingly endless energy. Lack of movement is often associated with decline or illness.

Adults often need motivation to move with anything more than a casual effort.

If motivation is important to peak physical performance, should we not consider how important it is to faith development? Are we motivated to offer God our best, or do we settle for casual effort?

In his book *Drive,* Daniel H. Pink explains that early humans were motivated by their strong need for survival. As civilization progressed, we developed various forms of cooperation and negotiation. The industrial era ushered in the reward-and-punishment model of motivation that continues to prevail today. We use it in our homes and in our schools as we prepare children to be responsible adults.

Pink suggests that a different kind of reward is gaining traction as a motivating factor. That reward is the intrinsic satisfaction we derive when we pursue purposeful and gratifying activities. He cites Wikipedia, the online encyclopedia produced by volunteer contributors, as one example. Thousands of people from all walks of life share their expertise with no compensation and no recognition. They contribute to the world of open-source information for the simple satisfaction of knowing they played a role in its production and in the accumulation of knowledge in the world around them.[7]

I agree with Pink about the importance of intrinsic motivation, but I believe it's been around a long time. People have always volunteered for activities, with no reward other than the joy and satisfaction of contributing to something they value. Consider the closing ceremonies for the Sochi

Winter Olympics and the five thousand Russian volunteers who rehearsed routines for months in order to be part of that extravaganza.

Volunteer organizations benefit many. The Girl Scouts, American Cancer Society, Special Olympics, Knights of Columbus, and Red Cross are just a few of these—all volunteer based and affecting millions of lives.

While reward, punishment, and intrinsic satisfaction are established and well-known motivators, there is a greater motivator: signs. Whether we call them hints, cues, intuition, or divine revelations, we all rely on signs for direction and guidance. We especially rely on them when we find ourselves at one of life's crossroads.

Signs have effectively changed the course of history. One noteworthy example occurred in AD 312, when Christians were being persecuted and martyred. The Roman Emperor, Constantine, was facing a crucial battle at the Milvian Bridge outside of Rome. His troops were outnumbered, and he faced the almost certain prospect of a crushing defeat. Accounts differ, but they essentially describe a dream or vision Constantine had prior to battle. He saw a cross of light with the words "With this conquer."

Constantine accepted this as a divine message. He immediately ordered his troops to adorn their shields and flags with the cross. With that sign leading the way, he rode into battle and won.

In gratitude, Constantine ended Christian persecution, recognized the legal status of Christians, built churches, and by these and other acts contributed to the spread of

Christianity as the dominant religion of the Roman Empire. I am struck by the directness of God's intervention and the impact it had on the spread of Christianity.

What and where are the signs in my life? How many times has there been a sign put clearly in my path, and I passed it by without the slightest recognition? Signs, internal and external, tell us how we feel, help us make decisions, and provide direction when we are lost. If you are married, think of the signs that helped confirm that your spouse was the right person for you. If you have purchased a house or a car, did you receive a sign regarding which to buy?

Signs are everywhere; there are so many, in fact, that they can be paralyzing as well as helpful. How do we identify the signs that are important to our life's purpose? A powerful question helps us sort through and focus on the ones that are right for us.

Sojourner Truth was an abolitionist and women rights' advocate who read signs with the utmost clarity and then acted on them with righteousness. Born into slavery in 1797, Sojourner was promised her freedom when she turned twenty-nine, but later her owner changed his mind. Sojourner Truth read his deceitfulness as a sign that she was no longer obliged to his servitude. Years later she explained, "I did not run off, for I thought that wicked, but I walked off, believing that to be all right."[8]

In 1851 Sojourner Truth stood before a women's rights convention and declared her powerful question four times in an ever more forceful voice: "Ain't I a woman?" In that same speech, she asked, "If my cup won't hold but a pint, and yours holds a quart, wouldn't you be mean not to let me have my little half-measure full? And if you have any intelligence, please don't answer 'I don't know.'"[9]

Sojourner Truth's powerful question continues to reverberate today, in a world where Black and Brown people are still subject to unequal treatment. And her question is especially agonizing for women. Recent events in Afghanistan remind us that some countries continue to deny women many human rights, including the rights to education and to employment.

What signs do we see regarding our faith? What signs do we ignore?

I have never met a person who did not experience signs, but many write them off as coincidence. It reminds me of the man caught in a flood who refused help from people who came by in a boat. He told them he expected God to save him. Eventually he drowned, and at the pearly gates, he confronted God.

"Why didn't you save me?" he asked.

God answered, "I tried to. I sent a boat."

Count on Intuition

Intuition is a bodily sensation, like the alarm that goes off when we approach the edge of a cliff or the "rightness" we feel when we find the perfect house or car to buy. We rely on those feelings, and we trust at those times when we know just which route to follow. I experienced that sort of knowing when I decided to return to school at age forty-seven.

Maya Lin, the designer and architect I introduced earlier, is renowned for her enormous intuitive ability. She describes the place intuition plays in her work: "My creative process balances analytic study, based very much on research, with, in the end, a purely intuited gesture. It is almost as if after months of thinking I shut that part of my brain down and allow the nonverbal side to react."[10]

Intuition leads to "What if . . . ?" questions. These are the light-bulb moments that most of us experience and then dismiss as impractical, too simple, or too big. Ray Kroc, the man who franchised McDonald's, helped redesign the American eating experience by asking himself if he could bring fast food into restaurants. More important, could he reproduce the dining experience, maintaining every standard of consistency and quality, over and over, across the country and then the world? Others might have eventually developed a similar concept, but he asked the question and then made it happen.

The iconic furniture designers Charles and Bernice "Ray" Eames, a husband-and-wife team, applied similar principles to modern furniture. They asked themselves what made sitting in a chair comfortable, and thus we have the Eames lounge chair and the Eames dining chair. What would happen if we were to ask parishioners what makes being Catholic comfortable—or uncomfortable?

An aspect of a powerful question that bears further exploration is its potential impact on management and human resources. If we know a person's powerful question, we know their intuitive lens. When choosing key personnel for a project, wouldn't it be useful to know not only an individual's talents and expertise but also their passion and purpose?

A world-class design team harnesses the creative synergy of multiple, complementary intuitive lenses. What if bishops asked priests to identify their most powerful question before assigning them to a particular parish? What if pastors asked lay ministers the same before assigning them to a parish team or responsibility?

Will Wright is the creator of *The Sims* and fifteen other video games that have sold over two hundred million units to date. Wright and his team developed an "infinitely flexible" game world. In an interview with Chris Baker for *Wired* magazine in August 2012, Wright explained that the common thread in his inventing career is the question "How can you give players more creative leverage and let them show off that creativity to other people?"[11]

Should we ask Catholics how we can give them more creative leverage in reaching out to those who have left the Church? And isn't that part of what Pope Francis is doing with his emphasis on synodality?

Abraham Maslow, one of the founders of humanistic psychology, was curious to find out why more people did not suffer from mental disorders. His question, "What is normal?" led to a more holistic view of human behavior. Humanistic psychology acknowledges the interconnectedness of mind, body, and spirit; it moves us away from a mechanical view of human nature. Maslow's theories can also help us understand that we all have potential for self-actualization.[12]

What if we asked Catholics what self-actualization means in their faith life? In fact, doesn't that offer another definition of a saint: one who lives up to their potential as a child of God?

Alan Turing, a pioneer in the science of algorithms (think Google search), helped break the Enigma code the Nazis used in World War II. He realized that humans working with paper and pencil would never be able to decipher the code, which changed daily. He visualized a machine that could process information regardless of the amount of data or complexity. His powerful question, "How can we get a machine to think?" led him to create a machine that recognized patterns. Turing's computer prototype cracked the code and was eventually credited with shortening the war by two years, saving as many as fourteen million lives.[13]

What patterns can we recognize in our life? Are these patterns adaptable to a life that changes daily? Our powerful question is likely embedded in those patterns—especially in patterns that are not adaptable, those that keep us stuck in some fashion.

To Live Authentically

Parents and teachers tell us we are special and unique, and we hear the word "authentic" a lot. That word means living without pretense, honoring and speaking the truth. But how many of us take the time to explore our uniqueness, and how many of us live a life that honors what is authentic about ourselves? That exploration is often set aside as we deal with societal expectations and our desire to fit in. Finding our powerful question is the deliberate way to interrupt the steady noise our culture produces and to see with new eyes what is authentic in ourselves.

What does a life that honors what is unique and special in ourselves and in others look like?

For starters, it is giving ourselves permission to say no and to choose how and when we will give of ourselves. This can appear selfish, but in fact, authentic people tend to give more because they have more to give. They choose their priorities and engage fully. Authentic people are open to the truth about their life. They embrace their special-ness as well as their vulnerability. This occurs naturally for those who are grounded in truth and who follow their powerful question.

Authentic people actively respond to life's offerings. This goes way beyond choosing a favorite restaurant or fashion statement. It is embracing, honoring, and developing one's own nature rather than trying to blend in. It is choosing to act ethically and morally, not because of guilt or fear of punishment but because doing so is consistent with the person God wants to hold close for all eternity.

Living authentically means accepting the paradoxical nature of life. We are strong, and we are weak. We are brave, and we are afraid. Living authentically means tak-ing risks and giving ourselves permission to be wrong as well as right, because anything less limits our possibilities. It means draining every last drop from our cup, whether that be half-full or half-empty.

Authenticity means being aware that our boundaries are cocreated limits and possibilities. They define our space and establish our zones of relationship. It means understanding that we need limits in order to have possibilities.

Think of children who have no rules and no one willing to stop them from acting impulsively. How are they to grow into responsible adults who know how to respect others? Feeling one's limits is basic to feeling alive, safe, and able to reach beyond.

Meeting our boundaries is meeting our truth. Living life in the middle gives us the illusion of being safe, but it restricts our possibilities of discovering who we are and what we are made for.

The Bible is full of parables in which Jesus challenges us to leave the comfort and safety of the middle. Whether you are Christian or not, these are instructive tales. For instance, there's the Good Samaritan (see Luke 10:25-37), who confronted cultural prejudices and social norms by stopping to help a stranger. Who hasn't known a Good Samaritan, and who would not agree that the world needs more of them? We can all live with that grace and courage.

?

CHAPTER FIVE

A Diamond You
Hold in the Light

*You don't want a million questions as much as you want
a few forever questions. The questions are diamond you
hold in the light. Study a lifetime and you see different col-
ors from the same jewel.*

—Richard Bach[14]

"A diamond you hold in the light" describes the essence of a powerful question. Embedded in our life story and our behavior patterns, a powerful question is what we love and what we fear. Unearthing this diamond ignites our passion and reveals our purpose. It moves us beyond ourselves and ushers us into our place in God's plan.

We live in a world that insists we choose sides—a world where religious affiliation, skin color, political party membership, and ethnic background are used as cause for all manner of injustice, and asking questions is dangerous. In many regions, asking questions is risking your life, especially if you are a journalist. At the end of 2020, Reporters Without Borders documented 937 journalists murdered in the past decade and 54 being held hostage in various locations. In addition, 387 journalists were detained, primarily in government-controlled prisons.[15] A world that murders or locks up journalists for asking questions is a world that cannot tolerate freedom.

Dangerous Questions

Edith Stein was a German-born Jew who converted to Catholicism and went on to become a cloistered Carmelite nun. She was arrested by the Nazis and sent to Auschwitz, where she died in 1942. The Catholic Church canonized her a saint and martyr in 1998. These facts make her life and death remarkable enough, but she is also recognized for her philosophical work in the field of phenomenology.

The phenomenological method studies how we know something and what that knowing means. Working closely with Edmund Husserl, the founder of phenomenology, Edith Stein wrote a dissertation, "On the Problem of Empathy," that is considered a bedrock study in her field. In her era, "problem" was another word for "question."

The powerful question that propelled Edith Stein's work was "What is empathy?" Her effort was to explain how a person can truly feel what another person is feeling. Her work was an obvious counterpoint to the absence of empathy at that time in Nazi Germany. Sadly, that question is still relevant today, in a world that grows increasingly hostile and disconnected.

As a child growing up in the 1950s, I would listen to my father and my uncle talking in their native Ukrainian tongue. I didn't understand a word. This was during the Cold War, and my father refused to talk about "the old country." One day I asked my uncle why all the secrecy.

My uncle put his finger to his lips and explained that it was dangerous to talk about the Soviet Union, even though it was far away. He explained that my grandfather had been locked in a Russian concentration camp, and he himself had spent time in a labor camp. He told me it was better not to ask questions or talk about it, because we still had relatives who lived in Eastern Europe, behind the Iron Curtain.

More recently, the coronavirus pandemic has had an impact on all of us. As we were forced to isolate and define what is essential, Edith Stein's powerful question about empathy called out in a loud voice. As the days and weeks dragged on, we began to understand that the real challenge was not only the virus but also people—people we did not even know but on whom our life depended. We stood behind masked people in the supermarket checkout line and jumped at the sound of a cough.

Whether it was because of the grocery clerk, the nurse, or the person walking by wearing a facemask, we began to experience a new kind of empathy. All of a sudden, needing each other to stay healthy was not just a nice sentiment. Their health directly affected our health, and this brought many of us together in understanding how fragile life is. We shared empathy and compassion with families whose loved ones died alone, in an isolation room at a hospital their family could not enter and with a funeral many could not attend.

A Healing Question

In response to tragedy, a powerful question is often a catalyst for healing. No one epitomizes that more for me than Elizabeth Bettina. Elizabeth is a native New Yorker who, as a youth, spent summer vacations visiting her grandmother in Campagna, Italy. The summer visits produced wonderful memories, and she continued to visit as often as she could as an adult.

During one such visit, Elizabeth was in a restaurant and spotted an old photo in a book chronicling the people and historical events of Campagna. What struck her about the photograph was the smiling rabbi, smiling priest, and smiling police officer standing next to one another. Jewish rabbis, Catholic priests, and police officers enjoying one another's company during the occupation of Italy in 1940 seemed so incongruent that she felt compelled to ask, "How did they get there? And why were they together?" Elizabeth's curiosity was heightened because she knew the picture was taken on the steps of the church where her grandmother was both baptized and married.

In her book *It Happened in Italy,* Elizabeth writes, "Little did I know that this discovery would change not only the course of my life, but many other lives."[16] Searching for an answer to her questions, she travelled the globe and interviewed hundreds of Holocaust survivors. She discovered that thousands of the Jewish people who fled Germany, Poland, and other occupied countries during that period had made their way to Italy. By 1940, when the photo of the priest, rabbi, and police officer was taken, Fascists had already established confinement camps in Italian towns.

Local citizens, however, quietly resisted. At great personal risk, they helped save many Jewish "visitors" living in their towns. They believed that Jewish immigrants should be treated as respectfully as any neighbor in need. Even police officials routinely risked their lives to help Jews avoid roundups.

Elizabeth's journey led to the publication of her book, along with work on a motion picture related to it titled *My Italian Secret: The Forgotten Heroes* (2014). Her work chronicles the stories of survivors and their families who, with Elizabeth's help, were introduced to the courageous Italians who saved their parents and grandparents. Her powerful questions, activated by a photograph in a restaurant, rippled a wave of healing that travelled across continents.

Overcoming Question Anxiety

Questions have been around since Adam and Eve, and some people declare that there are no new or original ones. This opinion sometimes quiets our anxiety, quells dissent, and keeps us in the land of what we already know instead of what we could know.

In reality, a question is new when we, as individuals, ask it for the first time. And it is powerful when it provides new connections or insights that lead to God's truth and our place in his plan.

Questions come in many forms, depending on their intended purpose. Some questions are meant to convey judgment: "Why are you friends with her?" or "What do you see in him?" Some questions are meant to impose order and authority: "Who gave you permission to do that?" Others are socially neutral and nonjudgmental, communicating a friendly attitude: "What do you think of this weather?"

Questions are also useful tools for selling merchandise or services. But such questions can be risky. Every salesperson has a story about an occasion when a poorly timed or inappropriate question cost them a sale.

Questions also have a dark side: intentionally or not, they can cause a person to feel anxious, guilty, or ashamed. Like many adolescents, I was introduced to question shaming as it slid down the piercing look my teacher gave me when I raised my hand too many times. I confess I was slow in picking up on these nonverbal messages, but gradually I learned that if I asked too many questions or the wrong kind of questions, the teacher considered me a nuisance. The message was loud and clear: "Don't ask questions."

I also learned early on that if the teacher asks you a question and you don't know the answer, it's better to give a vacant look and keep quiet than to persist in trying to find an answer. And never, ever answer a question with another question. That could mean a trip to the principal's office. I would suggest that question anxiety is firmly embedded in each of us by the time we graduate from high school.

Years back, I taught an introduction to psychology course at a community college. Each semester I assigned the students one short paper to write. They had to formulate a question relevant to their life and connected to human behavior. Their question had to be genuine, one they truly didn't know the answer to and one they were willing to explore. They didn't have to arrive at an answer in their paper; they simply had to develop a good-faith plan to pursue an answer.

Over the course of three semesters, there were students who suffered severe anguish over this assignment, and a few went so far as to suggest it was unfair. They said they needed a specific topic in order to write a paper and complained that I must be trying to trick them. Some felt it was impossible because they could look up answers to any question by reading a journal or searching the internet.

Each semester, however, a few brave, trusting souls took a chance and produced genuine questions. Those courageous students often thanked me later for introducing them to a new way of thinking about their life and purpose. I remember one young man who wanted to find out what it was like to live with attention deficit disorder. His brother was diagnosed with the condition, and he wanted to know out of a sense of compassion. (He received an A.)

In life we are taught to be tidy and wrap things up without leaving loose ends. That's why questions without apparent, readily understood, and verifiable answers usually end up relegated to the realm of philosophy or religion. Philosophers are allowed to pursue ideas that have no empirical proof, and theologians can use their "it's a matter of faith" card. We as Catholics, however, should realize that asking questions and seeking answers deepen our faith. God has the answer to any question we have the courage to ask.

Still, let us acknowledge that questions without clear and accessible answers make us uncomfortable. We sometimes cope with this discomfort by deciding that a question is either irrelevant or unimportant. We might even dismiss it as an unanswerable riddle, such as "If two hands clap and make a sound, what is the sound of one hand clapping?" Who wants to spend time bothering with that?

But there are notable figures who have been unaffected by question anxiety and have turned questions into an art form. Michael Moore, the filmmaker, is both an overachiever and an inspiration in this regard. His 1989 film *Roger and Me* documents his attempts to get General Motors Chairman Roger B. Smith to visit Flint, Michigan, and see firsthand the devastation caused by the closure of GM plants. Moore's persistence in pursuing Mr. Smith—in order to ask him simple, direct, and to-the-point questions—established him as a new force in documentary filmmaking. Asking candid questions in a naïve and disarming manner produces a special brand of humor. Moore engages viewers with this format and lures them into new and sometimes startling realizations.

The Importance of Questions

Even with all their baggage, questions are an important part of everyday life. In the business world, questions are a way to determine value and assess productivity. Employers ask questions to determine whether employees are meeting goals, and employees are expected to have the answers. Good salespeople ask good questions before they decide whether to try to sell you something.

In social situations, asking questions can signify care and concern, as in "How are you?" or "Did you sleep well?" Inquisitiveness can be a polite form of interacting without revealing one's position or level of commitment. Socially acceptable questions can be useful ways to gain information and create a favorable impression.

Questions as simple as "Where did you get that scarf?" can lead to a discussion about color choices, values, and lifestyle. These curiosity questions invite engagement and conversation. They're safe ways to test the water and determine the possibility of a deeper relationship.

Questions also establish compatibility by determining mutual interests. "Did you catch that game?" "Do you believe the way that referee called a foul with three seconds left?" "Did you see those protesters last night on the news? What is wrong with them?" How the other person responds will tell you a great deal about and sometimes determine potential for relationship. This is socialization 101.

We might call close friendships socialization 102. And what better way to tell if a relationship is close than by the fact that we can ask personal questions without being uncomfortable? Personal questions tend to happen only in situations where trust is established.

Does that not also apply to our relationship with God?

CHAPTER SIX

When Is a
Question Powerful?

A question is powerful when it reveals meaning and purpose. Viktor Frankl, a psychiatrist who survived imprisonment in the Nazi death camp Auschwitz, wrote about his ordeal in *Man's Search for Meaning*. He credited one factor above all others as key to survival in those conditions. That factor was finding some meaning and hope in what the person had to endure.[17]

Frankl proposed that the search for meaning is a primal quest. An endless stream of selfies and inspirational quotes on social media give the impression that many people today are pursuing meaning, but more "likes" do not produce more meaning. More meaning comes from asking ourselves what we need and long for the most. Answering that question is worth a thousand selfies.

A powerful question reveals what is present in our life but not fully recognized. Our memory records special events, such as birthday parties, touchdowns scored, and first loves. A powerful question is embedded not so much in our memory of the events, which fades over time, as in the interpretations we assign to them. We weave these interpretations into our story, our narrative, and then integrate them into our ways of acting and reacting.

Over time and with enough repetition, these interpretations form our beliefs, expectations, and even our identity. Examples might include "I work best under pressure" or "I'm never lucky." They also become internalized as our basic understanding of "This is who I am."

Children receive hundreds if not thousands of messages. Some are positive, as in "You have a way with words" and "You have a gift for music." Some are negative, as in "You never finish what you start" and "Don't even try; that's not for you."

Like a continuous loop of background music, messages received during childhood can continue to play in our subconscious. Positive messages are sources of motivation and strength, while negative messages produce feelings of inadequacy. A powerful question exposes these messages for what they are and enables us to let go of negative self-judgment.

When a Powerful Question Transforms

A most powerful question is life changing and transformative. It shakes us awake with a new awareness of ourselves. Just as a butterfly cannot change back to a caterpillar, we are not able to return to who we were before we found and awoke to our powerful question.

Laura MacDonald, an early participant in my powerful question classes, is justifiably proud of her reputation as a "people connector," someone who links those in need with those who can help. Initially she resisted the idea of having to arrive at only one powerful question. She owns a successful business and enjoys a diverse mix of friends and activities. Her life was filled with new possibilities, and she feared that having only one question would be limiting. If it had to be just one, she felt it should be "What's next?"

What finally struck a chord with Laura was the concept of legacy. That came to her when she happened across an attic full of one family's historical data in an abandoned building she was renting. At the turn of the twentieth century, a family with eleven children owned the building in Negaunee, Michigan, and ran a department store in it. Strangely enough, there were no living heirs, and no one wanted the storehouse of letters, picture albums, and keepsakes.

Laura felt drawn to the mystery of this family with no heirs. She began to examine documents and letters that explained the family's history. Over the course of two years, she discovered that they were Jewish immigrants from

Russia who had thrived but then seemingly disappeared from the face of the earth.

The more Laura learned, the more connected she felt to this family and the concept of legacy, how it happens, and how it can disappear. This raised questions about her own ancestry. It was no surprise when "What is legacy?" emerged as her powerful question. That question continues to lead her to new insights. She is now working on a book about her "adopted" family, one filled with intrigue, question marks, and even a ghost.

Laura's legacy question transformed her life beyond anything she could have imagined. Today her life is still marked by connection, but she reports a stronger, deeper spiritual aspect that's visible to all who know her.

Another Healing Question

As noted previously, a most powerful question is often the impetus for healing. Another Laura, Laura Kelly, joined the powerful question family in 2013. At that time, she was sixty-two, retired, and feeling rudderless. She had always had a surplus of energy, but she felt beaten down by chronic pain and fatigue due to fibromyalgia and thirty-two years of caring for children as an advocate in the juvenile justice system. The "warrior woman" drive she always counted on was missing, and she feared it might be gone for good.

Laura was already reflecting on her life and the changes she seemed to be undergoing when she began the journey to find her powerful question. The question that emerged for her was "How do I regain my warrior energy to make positive change?" In 2017 I asked her to speak to the changes she experienced as she searched for an answer.

I started my quest by trying to combine my own spirituality with the act of exercising. I saw the movie titled The Way, *starring Martin Sheen, and this became the catalyst to attempt to walk the four-hundred-mile pilgrimage known as the Camino de Santiago (the Way of St. James) across the northern part of Spain. I became engrossed in studying the history of the Camino and discovered it was once an ancient Roman trade route. In the two years that followed, I began mapping out the route and learning about the towns and villages and the miles between them. I saw videos about the Camino, read books, and listened to a lecture by a woman about my age who had walked the entire route herself. I had never been on a pilgrimage, and there was plenty of testimony that this one was a very spiritual experience for those who learned to walk in a deeper way.*

I purchased boots and special walking poles to help steady myself and support my weakened leg muscles and worn joints. I started to walk the northern trails that are plentiful in my hometown. Over time, I hiked as much as the long Upper Peninsula of Michigan winters and my pain endurance would permit. I was trying to condition myself so that I could walk as many miles as possible along the Camino. This structured physical conditioning was the first since my fibromyalgia emerged in 1987.

My powerful question led to answers and still more questions. "What if I hike a long distance even though I suffer from chronic pain?" "Could I experience a spiritual awakening through this pilgrimage?" "What does it mean to walk in a deeper way?"

In May of 2016, plans had been finalized and nonrefundable tickets purchased to make the thirty-one-day trek along the Camino de Santiago. The only thing left to do was complete a physical and have a routine colonoscopy before I made the trip. Two weeks before I was due to start my pilgrimage, I received a call from the physician who performed the colonoscopy and was informed that I needed surgery right away for colon cancer. He strongly advised me to cancel my trip to Spain.

The news of this second bout of cancer within two years was at first startling but not as disappointing as the thought of cancelling my Camino trek. However, as the news settled in, I had a different mindset than I had with my first battle with cancer two years prior. There was within me a kind of strength and optimism that I had not experienced in a long time. I felt the emergence of my warrior self.

When I met with the surgeon, I shared that the doctor who gave me the colonoscopy advised the immediacy of the surgery. Undaunted, I asked my surgeon, "Do you think that I can postpone the colectomy to walk eight days of the thirty-one-day pilgrimage in Spain?" After much discussion, the surgeon agreed there was little risk in postponing the operation for a short window of time so that I could walk some of the Camino.

After experiencing a small part of the pilgrimage as well as undergoing a successful colectomy, I realized I had already undergone a transformation. My powerful question had become the lightning rod to commit mind, body, and spirit to meeting the health challenges I was experiencing. In pursuing my powerful question, I had learned to walk in a deeper and more determined way. I had become unstuck from the myriad of miseries that plagued my former self. I found my warrior energy to walk with chronic pain and keep walking. I became energized and confident to undergo cancer surgery and treatment twice in two years with a strength I thought I had lost. I also discovered that I could have deep spiritual connections by hiking the trails back to my warrior self.

In the summer of 2016, Laura finally completed the Camino with her sister, niece, and daughter. While training for that walk, she felt her old vitality begin to return.

When a Powerful Question Gives Us Focus

A powerful question can be a lens that not only gives us focus but also keeps us focused.

I met Patty when she attended a powerful question retreat I conducted for lay ministers in the Archdiocese of Milwaukee. Patty is active in her parish, a former probation officer, and a seamstress who enjoys making wedding dresses for young women who can't afford them. Her question, "How does this all fit?" incorporates her experience as a seamstress. It is very visual and connected. Her words describe the focus it provides:

As far back as I can remember, I have been intrigued by the living God and, on multiple levels, aimed to love the Lord with my whole heart, my whole soul, and my whole mind. How is that possible when a person feels, more often than not, fragmented and adrift, equipped with an out-of-focus lens that skews clarity?

Just prior to my sixteenth birthday I had a unique sense of expectation. Something good was just around the corner. Several months later, when praying with others, I had a laser-focused Epiphany. "God knows my name!" WOW!

This was hot off the press for me, and it was the best news ever! He knew everything about me and loved me unconditionally. He delighted in me! He knew me inside and out and found me lovable! The certainty of this revelation transformed my life.

I belonged. I was connected. I fit in.

However, I was not shielded from making many mistakes in thought, word, and deed. I did not always live the transformed Christian life, and I closed some doors to the Lord where I wasn't comfortable letting his light shine.

The ragtag, well-intentioned assortment of fragments that were my life moved about as in a kaleidoscope—presented as beautifully arranged one minute but, with the turn of the wheel, not so much.

The Lord never gave up on me, and I never shunned his gaze long-term. His word has been my source of nourishment, consolation, strength, healing, and light.

When I came to the retreat for pastoral associates facilitated by Dr. O, I was "prayed up" and prepared to dig deeper. When I uncovered my powerful question, "How does this all fit?" I felt contentment.

The feeling in my innards was that "It is well with my soul." This question turned my gaze.

My question has enabled me to lovingly nudge out of and negate the long-embedded sense that I "don't fit," that I "don't belong."

Conversely, it has sharpened focus on identifying things, through discernment, that I perceive as divine inspiration and those things that don't fit: hatred, injustice, evil, victimization, prejudice, stinking thinking, etc.

Since finding my powerful question and through the COVID quiet, I've found contentment and consolation in the Holy Spirit.

My powerful question promotes my desire to love God with my whole heart, my whole soul, and my whole mind. Fragments can fit. Fit happens.

When a Powerful Question Lets the World Know Who We Are

A powerful question declares that our life has meaning. Like all heroic journeys into the unknown, ego and expectations take a back seat. Public declaration of our question compels us to go forward and discover our truth and our purpose. Turning back is not an option.

Initially I found this aspect of my powerful question terrifying. I had a long history of avoiding the spotlight and staying in the background. Growing up in a large family, I found that this strategy helped me avoid unwanted scrutiny—as well as chores.

Declaring a powerful question makes us vulnerable in a unique way, a little like a person wearing a religious habit or a clerical collar. Our identity is clearly out in the open, and others are free to judge. Yes, declaring a most powerful question will bring judgment from those who want to judge. But above all else, we will be judged as someone who believes their life has meaning and purpose. And as our question touches on and propels our faith journey, it will touch others as well.

"What is boundary?" is my powerful question. What does that say about me?

Some might hear this as a personal issue. Others may judge my question (and me) to be "much ado about nothing." After all, we all know what a boundary is, right? Castle walls and picket fences have been around for a long time. Because boundary is so utilitarian and taken for granted, we seldom think about it until it's violated—when, for instance, a person is rude or cheats us in some way.

In fact, boundary is the relational space we cocreate with others all day, every day. It is space we negotiate and navigate as we feel our effect on others and their effect on us. This is a skill set we learn as children, when the words "yes" and "no" teach us our limits as well as our possibilities. If our boundaries are poorly formed, we are at the mercy of each new set of circumstances. Healthy boundaries are a necessary precondition to feeling safe and open to God's embrace.

My most powerful question has brought new meaning and purpose to my profession as a psychologist. It also gives me the means to be a healing force in my Catholic faith (the duty of every baptized Catholic). Maintaining appropriate boundaries, as we are now all too aware, is a critical factor in the lives of healthy priests as well as healthy congregations. Personally, I appreciate my life in ways I never could before.

We have to let go of judgment, our own and others', and trust in the path that God lays before us. I firmly believe it is God who plants the powerful question in each of our life stories. And when we declare our question publicly, it invites others to find the most powerful question embedded in their life story.

Remember, this is new territory for most people, and that first step can be scary. "What if I fail?" "What if I don't like what I find?"

When a Powerful Question Welcomes a Person Home

Traveling with friends to the Disney resort in Orlando, Florida, I witnessed an encounter that left a strong impression. The staff at the front desk greeted my friends, who are members of the Disney Vacation Club, with a warm "Welcome home!" Such a simple thing and such a powerful way to say, "You belong; you are family; we have missed you." It made me think about the power of a greeting.

Imagine the impact that greeters in the back of church might have if they said, "Welcome home," instead of, "Good morning," as parishioners arrived for Mass. And isn't that more to the point of belonging to a parish? Could this be evangelization 101?

A powerful question speaks the same kind of invitation and belonging message. After I completed a consultation at a seminary, a priest drove me to the airport. When we arrived, we sat down for a cup of coffee before my flight. I began telling him about the powerful question ministry and about my own question; and finally, I asked him if he had such a question in his life.

As tears formed in his eyes and he stifled a sob, he said that for years he had indeed had such a question. It was this: "What can change my dysfunctional family?" Although I was certainly not evangelizing at that moment, I felt that by listening to him I was saying, "Welcome home." Sharing a question that has that kind of intensity is a homecoming experience, because it says we belong not only to ourselves but also to one another in a way that only family and life-long friends can understand.

This kind of "welcome home" message can be an evangelizing moment and even evangelization 101—the initial welcome we extend to others. A powerful question has enormous potential in evangelizing—not only to invite lapsed Catholics home but also to invite those without faith. It's also a tool for parish renewal. It reminds those already on the journey that they are family and loved as such.

What is evangelization except being the pebble that hits the water, creating ripples? The question we share and the question we ask could be pebbles that release a tsunami of faith. Yes, it is risky, but not as risky as not doing anything and watching our parish family dwindle.

When a Powerful Question Forces Us to Think on a Bigger Scale

We limit ourselves when we only engage with questions to which we can find answers. Easily solvable fact-finding exercises are not likely to produce transformative, break-through discoveries. In contrast, a powerful question allows us to set aside what we already know and open ourselves to the unknown.

One example: now that we are sending rockets into space on a regular basis, scientists are turning to the problem of fuel for interplanetary travel. The solution based on what we already know is to build fuel storage tanks on nearby asteroids or even on the moon. Some scientists now are asking a different question, one that is infinitely more challenging but with enormous potential. They are asking how we might turn asteroids into fuel stations by extracting fuel from the rock found there.

Questions without simple answers are questions worth asking. Your powerful question may initially be baffling, but it won't always be—especially if you ask God for his help in understanding its meaning and purpose. Prayer, as those of us who practice it know, does work. Prayer is recognizing that our intentional search for purpose is also a search for God.

?

CHAPTER SEVEN

Set the World on Fire

St. Catherine of Siena is responsible for the quote "If you are what you should be, you will set the whole world on fire."[18] A powerful question is the focused way to pursue "what you should be" and your full potential. The more we understand what "full potential" means, the better our chances of getting there.

Two notable authorities on that subject are Plato, the Greek philosopher, and Abraham Maslow, the psychologist and founder of humanistic psychology. Although separated by twenty-three hundred years, these two arrived at similar conclusions. Plato created a story, the allegory of the cave, to describe social restrictions and the perils of enlightenment. Maslow drew a pyramid to illustrate the hierarchy of human needs and what it means to stand at the apex.[19]

These illustrations contain similar cautions and predictions. Both help us understand what living up to one's potential means and what we might expect if and when we get there.

Plato's Cave

Plato's story, the allegory of the cave, appears in his classic work *The Republic*, written around 400 B.C. and still considered a foundation stone in classical education. Plato tries to describe social reality and what happens when someone attempts to live outside that reality. He imagines a world in which everyone lives in a cave in which they are chained to the walls. Because of their confinement, they see one another only as shadows cast by the light of a fire in the middle of the cave. This shadowy existence is all anyone knows, and they all accept it as the way life is.

Over the course of time, one cave dweller's chains become rusted and break apart. This man stumbles around and eventually finds an exit. Emerging from the cave, he is initially blinded and frightened by the bright sunlight. In time, however, he begins to appreciate light, warmth, color, and clarity.

Transformed and excited, the man rushes back into the cave to share his discovery with the others, fully expecting to be treated as a hero. Instead he is scorned and admonished to "stop talking such nonsense." He persists, and the threats begin: "Stop, or you will be banished." But he cannot stop. The freedom and the light are too compelling for him to stay silent. Eventually he is driven from the cave and warned that he will be killed if he dares return.

Does this story speak to twenty-first-century life? What are the shadows we take as our reality? Have certain individuals emerged from the cave, and have they been killed?

We have some persuasive evidence that the Rev. Dr. Martin Luther King, Jr., understood the truth of this allegory. He seemed to be saying as much in his now-famous "I've Been to the Mountaintop" speech, delivered shortly before he was assassinated: "Well, I don't know what will happen now. We've got some difficult days ahead. But it really doesn't matter to me now, because I have been to the mountaintop."[20]

An interesting footnote: Dr. King mentioned Plato by name earlier in this speech. This was hardly a coincidence. Dr. King was well-versed in the truth contained in Plato's allegory, and he had no illusions regarding his own fate.

What about Nelson Mandela in South Africa? He spent over twenty-seven years in prison for speaking out against apartheid. Heroically, he kept his mountaintop vision alive and emerged from the shadows of apartheid to give his entire country a new future filled with hope.

It could be said that Jesus Christ arrived on earth in order to redeem all cave dwellers. He delivered his own mountaintop speech, in which he predicted how his message of peace and love would be received. "Jesus said to them, 'The Son of Man is to be handed over to men, and they will kill him, and he will be raised on the third day'" (Matthew 17:22-23).

What does coming out of the cave and into the light of Jesus Christ, "light of the world," mean here? The apostles and martyrs knew very well what it meant. They found the light Jesus Christ offered so compelling that dying did not seem too high a price to pay. That is something worth thinking about!

Maslow's Pyramid

Twentieth-century psychologist Abraham Maslow proposed that we have basic needs that must be filled in order to have a meaningful, happy, and well-ordered life. He drew a pyramid with basic needs at the bottom and moving to higher needs at the top. As we meet basic needs, we are able to work on satisfying higher needs. Maslow's pyramid is appealing in its practicality and simplicity.

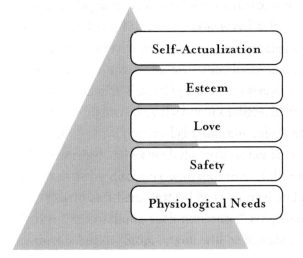

Physiological Needs

Infants have physical needs—for food, water, and air. This is obvious. Less obvious, but just as critical, is their need for physical touch and nurturing. These needs form the base of Maslow's pyramid. If these needs are unmet, it will be difficult, if not impossible, for children to survive, much less advance to higher needs. One tragic example of this is children in some orphanages who receive little human contact and suffer failure-to-thrive syndrome.

In line with Maslow's theory, the National School Lunch Program, launched in 1946, is one of the single most important contributions to the field of education in the past seventy years. And in 1966, the United States Department of Agriculture launched the National School Breakfast Program. In meeting a child's basic need for food, these programs recognize that a hungry child is not likely to absorb a great deal of math or English.

Safety

Safety is level two on Maslow's pyramid. I am reminded of the well-meaning uncle who, when I was quite young, tossed me up high, where I seemed to remain, suspended and terrified, in mid-air. Would he catch me on the way down? He did, but I avoided his reach after that.

Safety becomes more complicated and important as we grow, with multiple internal and external dimensions. Internal safety is reflected in our level of self-confidence and the extent to which we feel valued. External safety is knowing we have healthy, secure boundaries that protect and honor our needs while respecting the needs of others. We can never feel truly safe if we do not respect others. This has been well demonstrated by tyrannical dictators who must be constantly on guard even with members of their own inner circle.

Feeling unsafe is a breeding ground for anxiety. Efforts to control our environment and our circumstances are often efforts to feel secure and safe. Individuals with unmet safety needs may overreach and overcontrol in their efforts to feel safe. Compensating for unmet safety needs can undermine a person's ability to form healthy relationships. This is particularly true for individuals who have been abused or traumatized as children.

Safety is also the underlying issue attached to the ongoing sexual abuse scandal in the Catholic Church. Direction in maintaining the safety of children and vulnerable adults and in establishing good boundaries now receives the highest priority in ministerial formation. These issues are no longer taken for granted.

Love

Level three on Maslow's hierarchy is love. Love is an emotional awareness, which an infant first experiences while being held, seeing themselves reflected in their mother's eyes. If the infant sees love, they know themselves as lovable. If they see emotions such as worry, they might know themselves as something other than lovable. What they see and feel becomes the foundation for how they know themselves.

Love is the subject of movies, books, and songs. As the saying goes, love makes the world go round. Because of the complexity of emotions involved, not to mention hormones, love is easily the most discussed (and least understood) of human needs. Love can be platonic—felt deeply by family members and best friends—as well as romantic. It usually involves the expectations and needs of those involved.

There is a spiritual aspect to love that's hard to describe but seldom needs explanation. Virtually anyone who has ever been in love experiences this feeling of completeness and a return (if only briefly) to the inexhaustible source from which all love springs. We know there are limits to human love, but our Catholic faith teaches us that there are no limits to God's love.

Esteem

Feeling secure and loved allows children to move toward self-esteem as they reach adolescence. Self-esteem arrives most visibly in the preteen years, when friendships, loyalties, and popularity become paramount. In the teen years, young people pursue belonging and being included by joining cliques, clubs, and teams. Not belonging leaves them feeling excluded and not good enough.

Adults who struggle with low self-esteem are often their own worst enemy. They may have the skills and credentials to do their job, but they fail to advance or win promotions. They may be attractive as potential mates, but they fail to find the love they desire.

Feeling "not good enough" and "not deserving" can often be traced back to preteen experiences of rejection. The same less-than-good and undeserving feelings apply as well to those who suffered abuse in childhood.

Self-Actualization

The top rung on Maslow's hierarchy is self-actualization. While the first four levels are logical and almost a given, this fifth one can be perplexing. On the one hand, it is the highest potential we could hope for; but on the other hand, it can indicate that we are somewhat different and isolated. As the old saying goes, "It's lonely at the top."

According to Maslow, a certain amount of isolation is to be expected at the self-actualized level, because at that level, a person marches to the beat of their own drum. They don't look to others to determine the actions they will take. They have a moral and ethical compass that tells them what to do. They don't respond to crowd mentality or seek approval from others.

In his book *The Farther Reaches of Human Nature*, Maslow describes a self-actualized person as having meaningful connections, being able to act spontaneously, having a clear sense of what is true and what is false, and being free from social convention.[21] Maslow understood this to be rarefied territory, inhabited by the likes of Abraham Lincoln,

Albert Einstein, Eleanor Roosevelt, and others who possessed extraordinary levels of self-determination. I would certainly add Pope St. John Paul II to that list.

Lincoln, Roosevelt, and John Paul II are obvious examples, but is self-actualization a realistic goal for the majority of human beings? What kind of person is this going to be? Let me introduce you to someone who embodies a great deal of that characterization.

I first met Tonja when she approached me for licensure supervision in her work as a psychologist. Tonja's intelligence is in the superior range, and her therapeutic expertise is too. Her quest to understand the human condition began early in life. In college she wrote what was, at the time, an unconventional paper that examined gender roles and creativity.

Tonja has a successful private practice and enjoys a steady string of referrals from satisfied clients. After twenty-five years of study and practice in her field, she's still curious and excited about the issues her clients bring forward. She is exceptionally "present" and effective. No one would consider Tonja ordinary. I was pleased that she was willing to participate in the powerful question journey as both a participant and a cofacilitator.

Shortly after her involvement in powerful question classes, Tonja found her own question: "What is it to be authentic?" She remembers being drawn to the idea of living authentically during her teen years. Her powerful question helped her connect authenticity and self-actualization. She wanted to explore what it would be to consciously live in that space between authenticity and self-actualization, and she saw self-trust as critical to that process.

Tonja says that her question about being authentic has to do with self-awareness and transparency. She doesn't know what it would be like or what it would take to be authentic all the time, and she wants to find out. She believes the rewards will outweigh the vulnerability that might accompany living an authentic life.

Is Tonja self-actualized? When I asked her, she responded, "Yes, to the extent that I am committed to self-aware choices instead of anxious, awkward, neurotic self-doubt." I think Maslow would have applauded that answer.

Maslow cautioned that striving for self-actualization wouldn't necessarily lead to a contented or blissful life. Does that suggest that we should, in fact, be satisfied with achieving a measure of safety, love, and esteem? Many people appear to enjoy life to the extent that those needs are met. But is settling for this level of satisfaction contrary to our desire to be the best we can be?

Perhaps the story in Matthew's Gospel about the servant who buried his master's money speaks to this (see Matthew 25:14-30). It seems clear that God expects us to use the talents he has given us and, in praise and thanksgiving for these gifts, become the best we can be.

The Shared Message of Plato and Maslow

Plato and Maslow both portrayed an enlightened person as one who leaves the safety of the way things are and ventures into the unknown. Both men cautioned that there would be consequences for doing so. Going alone, and especially going ahead, is always risky. This was as certain in Plato's ancient Greece and Maslow's twentieth century as it is today.

In *Man's Search for Meaning*, Viktor Frankl shed light on the issue of self-actualization and what it takes to get there: "Self-actualization cannot be obtained if it is made an end in itself, but only as a side effect of self-transcendence."[22] Self-transcendence is traveling beyond the limits of what we know as "self" and into the mystery of God's truth and love.

That transcendence begins as a matter of course when we embrace our powerful question. The first step in this journey is wanting to know what is true and authentic about ourselves. Step two is finding our powerful question, the one that leads us out of the cave and into God's sunlight.

?

CHAPTER EIGHT

Steps to Your
Powerful Question

*The first step toward finding God, who is Truth, is to dis-
cover the truth about myself; and if I have been in error,
this first step to truth is the discovery of my error.*

—Thomas Merton[23]

Legend has it that an apple fell on Sir Isaac Newton's
head as he sat beneath an apple tree. That hit on the
noggin prompted him to ask, "Why doesn't the moon fall
from the sky?"

Whether Newton was hit by a falling apple or not, his
powerful question about the moon staying aloft was key

to unlocking the mystery of gravity. For those who lack an apple tree—or the time to sit under one—this chapter offers a deliberate approach to finding a powerful question.

There is no "one size fits all" route to a powerful question. Even with the benefit of the steps in this chapter, it's a self-directed process. You, the reader, must tailor these steps in a manner that honors you and your process. That includes stopping at any point if you feel overwhelmed and skimming over a step if you feel that doing so would serve you better. With that said, in my experience these steps have helped many engage in discernment of their most powerful question.

Each person's search will be unique. Some individuals arrive with a question they have carried silently in their heart for years and need only find their voice or a platform to speak it. Others may have a question they ask repeatedly but never stopped to figure out why. Still others may be intrigued by the idea of a powerful question but have fears and defenses that they must resolve before embracing it.

A Mini Review

As you begin this process, keep in mind some key points that we have considered in previous chapters. Remember: a powerful question tunes in to what is authentically and uniquely you. Your life is unique, not so much in the events—birthday parties, receiving good grades in math, first loves—but in the ways you interpret and derive meaning from those events. Over time these meanings merge with patterns of acting and reacting, and they are internalized. They are expressed in statements such as "I'm always late," "I'm always early," or "I can't stand conflict."

If repeated enough, these statements—self-judging as well as self-affirming—will evolve into life themes and patterns. These become the way we know ourselves and the way others know us, which are not always the same thing. Contained within these themes is a single question that will point us to our truth and our place in God's plan.

This journey is a form of prayer. Diane Scott—coach, writer, and Powerful Question Institute supporter—has found her powerful question: "What is legacy, and how do we create it?" As Diane's spiritual awareness has grown during this process, she connects her insight to powerful prayer and another powerful question: "What will I teach my grandchildren?" She writes:

Prayer takes many forms. It does not matter what your preference for prayer might be but simply that you do it. Do something prayerful every day. You will know it is powerful when it becomes constant, like breathing. Powerful prayer teaches patience and persistence. As God works through us, he teaches us faith and endurance. Prayer is not instantaneous or ASAP (as soon as possible) but ALAIT (as long as it takes) conversation. Powerful prayer requires the courage to wrestle with and do business with God every day, to have those daily conversations with God, to make those big requests. Powerful prayer helps us acknowledge both our blessings and our curses, to embrace the outcomes and the lessons that God has woven into our very own life journey.

Powerful prayer is accepting that God is there, working through us right now.

Powerful prayer will lead you to the heart of your powerful question. God is calling you to serve him. God has been ever present and embedded in your life story since the beginning. Powerful prayer will help you deepen your faith and strengthen your knowledge and acceptance of self. Developing a powerful prayer practice will lead you to discover and answer your unique calling to discipleship—and to find your powerful question. Conversely, pursuing your powerful question has the potential to bring you to a powerful prayer process.

Diane's explanation inspires and gives hope to those of us who want, more than anything else, to know we are walking the path with Jesus Christ. Pray that God will help you find the powerful question embedded in your life story. God will always answer powerful prayer.

You may be intrigued by the idea of a powerful question but dread the thought of having only one question. Don't let that stop you. Your question will evolve as you evolve.

A Question Renewed

Norma Semashko, a dedicated social worker with a long history of advocacy, attended a powerful question workshop a little over five years ago. The question she discovered, "What does it mean to be truly authentic?" sat on the shelf while her busy life continued. Then she reread my book *Ask Your Powerful Question* and sent me the following:

When I read the book again, I could feel an inner light pushing through to my awareness, and something awakened inside of me. It felt as if an inner voice were trying to guide me in my daily choices, and my decisions were aligning more with my values and beliefs. Listening to my inner voice allowed me to be vulnerable and openhearted. I started setting boundaries and walking away from toxic people and situations. I was more committed to standing up for my beliefs and especially my morals.

It felt as if my powerful question was renewing itself in my life. I realized new understandings and depth. As a result, my sense of purpose is now more present, and I am more aware of how choices I make reflect who I am and who I want to be. I hope and pray that I will continue on this path, regardless of who I may disappoint or how I am perceived by others.

Norma's experience is common. The powerful question that first arrives will show us more about ourselves and will become even more present over time, continuing to evolve. This is part of the transformation process.

It is critical, however, to have enough emotional space and peace of mind to engage in this discovery process. If you are dealing with some unresolved trauma, grief, or pain, your energy and focus are probably going there. The question that is likely to emerge will focus on the pain as opposed to you, the person experiencing the pain.

We all have wounds, but we are not our wounds. If your circumstance involves trauma, it might take some time for you to work your way around to a deeply satisfying powerful question.

A powerful question can center on a quest for personal growth and can draw on professional experience in a field of interest, such as science, philosophy, or the arts. Whether it appears to stem from personal or professional interests, the right question is one that connects with your life story and reveals your passion and purpose.

Steps

The following steps can help you find your powerful question. Your question may emerge quickly, or you may have to tease it out with help from a mentor or trusted friend. Rest assured, you will know it is the right question by the emotional and physical response it generates in you.

There are no time limits for going through these steps. For some people it takes days or weeks; for others, months or years. As we go through the steps, you'll use worksheets to help you focus your search for your most powerful question.

Here are the steps:

1. Create your personal timeline.
2. Create your faith journey timeline.
3. Identify ways you act, react, and cope.
4. Identify a prominent theme.
5. Identify what you do not know about that theme.
6. Verify your question with the involuntary physical/ emotional response.
7. Declare your question to the world.

Allow yourself time to engage reflectively in each step. Think of yourself as sort of a third-party observer and resist the urge to judge how you are progressing. Each step will provide its own insights. Another way to say this is "Trust the process."

Step 1: Create your personal timeline.

Identify important events in your life. These are the experiences that made a big impact on you, enough that they stand out among the thousands of other experiences you have had. Include the good ones as well as the ones you wish you could forget. You will want to record ten to twenty of the most significant events.

(Multiple births of children can be combined as one event, if that helps.)

1. Draw a single horizontal line. Start on the left with your earliest memory, and continue with events in chronological order until you arrive at the present. If any of these events bring up painful memories, please respect your emotional needs. This may be a signal that you have unresolved issues that you need to address. If so, make sure to take care of those needs.

2. When you complete your timeline, circle the events that stand out from the others and still have a strong bearing on who you are and the way you relate to others.

3. Review your timeline with a friend or mentor. Do the same events stand out to them?

Step 2: Create your faith journey timeline.

Draw another horizontal line, and on this one record your faith journey. Include times when your faith and relationship with God felt strong and hopeful, as well as times when it was troubled or plagued by doubt.

Step 3: Identify ways you act, react, and cope.

The nurturing and love we receive from our parents and care-givers shape us, laying the groundwork for how we perceive ourselves. As we grow and mature—and receive feedback from family, friends, teachers, and the world at large—our self-awareness continues to develop. Whether accurate or not, the messages we receive as children often become core beliefs about ourselves.

In this step ask yourself: when and how did I become aware of my talents and traits?

This step is an exercise in self-awareness. There are three parts, each with one or two worksheets to complete.

- On the first worksheet, you will complete sentences that reveal characteristics that may not always be on your radar.

- On the second worksheet, you will identify roles you play in different settings.
- Worksheets 3A and 3B reveal the "coping" section of step 3. Here you will identify the strategies you employ to cope with life's pressures and stress.

Worksheet 1: Sentence Completion

Resist the temptation to analyze the statements or present your ideal self as opposed to your authentic self.

1. A famous person I most admire is _____
because _____.

2. A famous person I least admire is _____
because _____.

3. I am happiest _____
because _____.

4. It really makes me mad _____
because _____.

5. My dream in life is _____
because _____.

6. My parents/caregivers expected me _____
because _____.

7. I reacted to my parents/caregivers' expectations _____
because _____.

Worksheet 2: Ways I Know Myself

Complete the "I am" statements to describe ways you act and react with your family, friends, peers, and authority figures at school, work, or home. These may include ways that have been pointed out to you by others.

In my family, I am _____

_____

_____

_____

_____

In school or work, I am _____

_____

_____

_____

_____

With my friends, I am _____

_____

_____

_____

_____

With authority figures, I am _____

_____

_____

_____

_____

When challenged, I am _____

_____

_____

_____

_____

I am happiest when I am _____

_____

_____

_____

_____

When I have a goal, I am _____

_____

_____

_____

_____

In private, I am _____

_____

_____

_____

_____

Coping Strategies

Now you will consider ways you cope with the demands of life and the stress these demands generate. Without coping strategies, daily pressures would be overwhelming. Our cultural tendency is to categorize coping strategies as either healthy—such as exercise or watching a funny movie—or unhealthy—such as binge eating or drinking alcohol excessively.

All coping strategies, healthy and unhealthy, start with positive intentions. But some coping strategies can lead to more stress than they set out to avoid, and all coping strategies exact a price over time. Below I've listed some unhealthy strategies with labels that describe the behavior. You may have other strategies and other labels. We all use such strategies at one time or another, and if repeated enough times, a particular strategy is likely to become a habit. The strategies all work, at least initially, to lower stress and alleviate anxiety.

If you are always late, it may be to avoid socializing with those who arrive early. If you avoid participating in competitive sports, it may be because you fear winning or losing. Your defense mechanisms may address needs that existed years ago but do not exist today. Have your needs changed but your ways of reacting stayed the same? On worksheet 3A, you will look at the underlying positive intentions of your coping strategies and styles.

There are positive coping mechanisms. My own include prayer and exercise. Worksheet 3B will examine the positive coping mechanisms that you employ. Here are the negative ones:

The Ostrich hides their head in the sand. This is not really true of the bird, but it is a well-known depiction of people who do their best to avoid facing reality. This style is also called "denial."

The Invisible Person becomes so absorbed in their work, their barn, or their garage that they are invisible to those with whom they live. This coping style often starts as a rationalization that this is the only way to get peace and quiet.

The Compartmentalist: Politicians have given us many scandalous examples. They tell themselves, "I may have engaged in behavior that is unsavory, unethical, or illegal, but that behavior is not me." They live as if they are a chest of drawers that open and close, each with a life of its own.

The Controller keeps anxiety at bay by keeping everything orderly and precisely arranged. This coping strategy can extend to relationships as well.

The Bottomless Pit needs to have the best and the brightest new thing, but it's never enough. Their hunger for more provides distraction and relieves anxiety—at least as long as it takes to unwrap their latest toy.

The Deflector projects judgment and blame on others. This keeps them from the anxiety of accepting responsibility for their actions.

The Porcupine has a prickly disposition that keeps others away and expectations low. They fear what could happen if others see who they really are.

The Stoic, a word often ascribed to the late Henry Ford II, is one who "never explains, never complains."

The Martyr never feels right receiving the best of anything, always deferring to the needs of others. Sacrifice is their way of life.

As you review this list, remember that no one could spend every living moment in a totally responsible, rational, and mature way. For one thing, that kind of life wouldn't include play, which by definition is often childlike but is nevertheless quite necessary for a balanced life. I want to emphasize again that every action we take or attitude we generate has, at least in the beginning, a positive intention.

I used to smoke cigarettes, and I assure you that I didn't start smoking because I wanted cancer. I started in order to be cool, to look mature, and to fit in with peers. This was my way to reduce teenage anxiety. Over time, of course, smoking turned against me and caused predictable outcomes, including bronchitis and shortness of breath. Thankfully, I quit smoking years ago.

Life comes with daily doses of stress and pressure as well as fun and excitement. Coping strategies are simply ways to defend ourselves, to reduce stress, and to pursue our positive intentions. As you complete the next two worksheets, remember that you might use more than one style, depending on circumstances. Which coping strategy appears most often and in more settings for you?

Themes might emerge, incorporating both direct and indirect coping strategies. They can become the ways we navigate life and relationships. They interact with values, goals, expectations, family roles, and our unique perspectives.

If you cannot identify with any of the coping strategies I've outlined, you may need to seek input from friends and family members who are willing and able to give you honest feedback.

Worksheet 3A: My Coping Strategies

Complete the table below by checking the yes or no column for each coping style as it relates to your life. At the bottom, add any other strategies that you can identify for yourself. Next to each style for which you checked yes, identify at least one underlying positive intention.

Style	Yes	No	Underlying Positive Intentions
Ostrich			
Invisible Person			
Compartmentalist			
Controller			
Bottomless Pit			
Deflector			
Porcupine			
Stoic			
Martyr			
Another style I see:			

Worksheet 3B: Healthy Strategies

What approaches help release you from stress? Complete the table below with examples of what you do in stressful situations.

Presure	Positive Outlet
Deadline at work	Exercise Leave my desk and go for a short walk to clear my brain

Step 4: Identify a prominent theme.

When you have completed your assessment of roles, coping styles, and positive intentions, it's time to identify the things that stand out and form your prominent life themes. A prominent life theme is a pattern of thinking, feeling, or acting around which you form much of your identity and personality. Think of it as the wire frame an artist uses to form a sculpture. It's not visible on the finished product, but it's there giving shape, substance, and expression.

In a similar way, we have a framework that holds us together, giving shape and form to who we are. Ironically, this framework is often more visible to others, who can see it in the ways we express ourselves. It may be less visible to us because we often focus more on our intentions than on our actions.

For instance, we may want to please someone, but we end up doing something that addresses our own desires, not theirs. This might be the case, for example, when a husband gives his wife a new fishing rod for Christmas. He tells himself that she'll love fishing, as he does, once she tries it.

Frameworks—or more precisely, themes—are present at work, at home, and in relationships. Consider these, for example. In our families, we all know who the caretaker is, the sibling Mom and Dad know they can count on to care for them later in life. At work we know the one who works well in a team, and we know the one who needs constant affirmation.

On worksheet 4, titled "Prominent Themes," refer to your previous worksheets and lifeline memories. Identify five themes or patterns that stand out. Try to include at least one that has been part of your life for many years and at least one that others have pointed out.

If your list of prominent themes identifies old wounds, traumas, or losses, remember that your wounds are not you but are what happened to you. Try to focus on the ways the wounds shaped you. If, for example, a person lost an arm in an accident, they may have grown stronger in some other ways, such as developing an independent spirit.

Likewise, resist the urge to make your ideal self your point of reference. Ideals can keep us stuck in images of what we "ought" to be or what we "should" be doing. The person behind that mask is the one who can find truth, meaning, and purpose.

Worksheet 4: Prominent Themes

Review your previous worksheets, and pick five themes that stand out as key to who and what you are.

Themes That Emerged
1.
2.
3.
4.
5.
Of the five themes above, pick the one that you believe has had the most impact on your life:

After you have identified a prominent theme that is important to who and what you are, it's time for the most critical step in this process. This step goes to the heart of a powerful question and may test your perseverance. Stay with it. Wanting to find your question is the best predictor that you will indeed find it.

Step 5: Identify what you do not know about that theme.

This step delivers the eureka moment, when your powerful question emerges from the prominent theme you identified in step 4. It may be about the theme itself, your connection to it, or something the theme triggers.

You can start by asking yourself when and why this theme first appeared in your life. Do you know the answer? If yes, then how does it still affect you? If no, how can you find out?

How does this theme affect others? What value does it hold for you? Do you know how to define that value? What parts of your life does this theme touch upon? Is it difficult to stay with either the theme or the questions that lie underneath? If so, it may be a sign that you have additional issues that need to be resolved.

Identifying what you do not know about your prominent theme can be difficult if you push to "make it happen." Most often, what you don't know will emerge in ways you can't predict. Be patient, and stay with the tension this "not knowing" creates. Let it simmer, and allow yourself the freedom to be curious about what's going on internally. Consider how this tension makes you feel and what it does to you. Ask a mentor to guide you, or ask a friend who has been through the process. And remember to ask God to help you see what you need to see.

If you stay with it and keep alive your desire to find your powerful question, it will emerge. You'll know when it's the right question; mind, body, and spirit will unite and send you clear confirmation. I cannot say it strongly enough; there is a 100-percent success rate for those who stay open to letting their powerful question arrive.

Nancy, an early participant in my powerful question classes, was impatient to find her powerful question. Her search involved twists and turns, a not uncommon experience in the discovery process, but she was motivated and wanted to discover her question quickly. A highly organized, optimistic, get-it-done kind of person, Nancy is a mother and entrepreneur with a history of accomplishment. She's owned a concierge service and has experience as a financial analyst with a property development company.

In her first month with the program, Nancy took an initial stab at her powerful question and arrived at "Why does sharing who they are create strength in some people and fear in others?" This was a good question, to be sure, but as she sat with it for a while, she decided that it didn't quite address what she felt on the deepest level.

Nancy next arrived at "Why do some people fear intimacy, while others reach for it?" Again, a great question, but it didn't bring forth the physical or emotional response she saw others in the program experience, and that bothered her.

Nancy immersed herself in the search for a third month. Here's what emerged: "How do I teach people to trust that optimism works?" It was clear that she had certain people in mind. She explained that she could not understand these people; neither did she know how to help them become optimistic. This felt like an affront to her belief system.

Building on the sentence structure of another participant's question, Nancy refined her question further: "What do I need to do to move beyond my own fear in order to help others trust that optimism works?" Good, but still no goose bumps.

Two months later, Nancy's powerful question arrived with goose bumps on both arms: "Is optimism real—and if so, how can I help people choose to live by it?" She was beaming as she announced that that was what she had been holding out for: a strong physical affirmation that this was indeed her powerful question. Nancy's question hints at why so many people are attracted to her energy and why she produces results that leave others shaking their heads in wonder.

Nancy measured whether or not she had reached her deepest level of engagement by whether or not she had a physical reaction. She tried out various questions until she found the one that produced the affirmation—the actual goose bumps she sought.

Your process will be uniquely yours. Nancy used a goal-directed approach, while Kurt, below, used almost the opposite approach. They started with different mindsets, and both were successful.

Kurt was a deeply spiritual graduate student, committed to a life of faithful service. He began his search for a powerful question with a mixture of skepticism and curiosity. He completed the first three steps and reported that he felt no closer to finding his question. I suggested he continue praying for guidance and that he avoid forcing it. A few weeks later, Kurt reported that he was still skeptical. After another week, having let go of any expectations, he had what he described as a transcendent experience.

One morning, after finishing his normal routine of morning prayer, Kurt was shaving when a bright light appeared in the mirror. At the same moment, his powerful question arrived, leaving no doubt in Kurt's mind that this was the one.

Many who discover their powerful question report that it arrived as if miraculously, after they stopped trying to force it into existence. What is the old saying? "Let go, and let God."

Step 6: Verify your question with the involuntary physical/emotional response.

The involuntary physical reaction—the goose bumps and bright light—that Nancy and Kurt experienced with their powerful questions provided the confirmation they needed. We can all expect involuntarily reactions when we first encounter our powerful question. It can be a sharp intake of breath, awkward laughter, or a feeling in the pit of one's stomach. These and many other reactions signal that the powerful question is emerging from the core of who we are.

My breathing stopped and I was speechless when Dr. Perry asked me where my boundaries were during our initial supervision session. Recognizing something at the core for the first time is a shock to the system. Interestingly, I still get a physical reaction when I encounter a boundary event. It is as if my internal alarm is always tuned to this possibility.

Not all powerful questions bring truly dramatic and gut-wrenching responses, but all are accompanied by an internal sign that signals this is the right question for you. These signs assure you that this is not just a mental exercise, like getting the right answer on a television quiz show. This is you, opening up and letting the light in.

Step 7: Declare your question to the world.

This step is your public commitment to the discovery process. Letting others know your most powerful question is empowering. Doing so invites others to hold you accountable and support you on your journey.

Would the person who decides to climb Mount Everest or take on some other formidable challenge keep it to themselves? Only if they are unsure about their commitment. Committed individuals seek out those who might support them in appropriate ways. They also seek out those who might be skeptical, just to test their own resolve. A powerful question is no less an endeavor than other formidable challenges and needs the same level of commitment and support.

Declaring our powerful question demonstrates humility and confidence: humility that we are beginning to know something vital about who we are, and confidence that what we discover is going to make a difference on a large scale. It's bold and risky, a little like the boast Thomas Edison made when he declared that his facility at Menlo Park would be an invention factory that would churn out new inventions every week.

If you're reluctant to tell others about your important question, it may be a sign that you're not sure your question is important enough. This is where a good support system can help you appreciate the value of finding your purpose in life. Powerful question workshops and classes provide an opportunity to present your question to others. Standing before peers and sharing your process and question is both affirming and humbling. We reveal who we are and what touches our life. We share what we want to discover and receive feedback and assistance in return.

Expect, however, that your friends—even your closest friends—may respond to your powerful question with a dismissive shrug or "What's the point?" Powerful questions can sound trivial to those who have not experienced life as you have or who have not pursued their own greater purpose. Accept the fact that others will not understand how potent a powerful question is until they experience it themselves or see what it does for you.

In the early days of my search for a definition of boundary, I was eager to get feedback from others; but most people responded with indifference. One instructor said that "boundary" was simply another word for "limit," and that ended the discussion, as far as he was concerned. His comment nearly stopped me from pursuing a definition.

Once you proclaim your powerful question and own it as yours, commit yourself to the search for an answer. This is not an idle commitment. Let your question lead you. And again, trust the process.

?

CHAPTER NINE

Pursuing an Answer

There is no single or right way to pursue an answer to your most powerful question. There is only your way—using your talents, gifts, and inclinations. Find this way that feels right for you, and trust that your question and your discoveries will evolve as you do.

Powerful questions lead each of us differently. I did a lot of soul searching and research and finally wrote a book about boundaries; Laura Kelly walked part of the Camino; and Laura MacDonald took at-risk youth on mountain-bike rides. Some people begin by researching the key words or topics in their question. Others enroll in school or immerse themselves in prayer, meditation, art, or music.

Your search will yield results if you persevere, but don't expect a final or complete answer. The benefits you derive as you travel this journey will be a hundredfold. Your journey may look difficult to those watching from the outside, but you'll live out what makes you passionate. And that, ultimately, is your answer: a life of purpose unfolding across the years as your question leads you in a multitude of ways to a multitude of situations and challenges.

A most powerful question isn't just for those who want to make some major breakthrough in science or business; it is for anyone who wants to honor the life they have and the God who gave it to them.

Shanedra is a lay minister for the Catholic Church in Milwaukee, Wisconsin, who enrolled in a master's degree course I was teaching at Sacred Heart Seminary. The powerful question she discovered was "Is the peace I know the peace I live?" I'll let her tell you about the process and what it has done for her:

Discovering my powerful question involved allowing myself to go to the inner me, well below the surface. I had to be vulnerable and honest with myself. I am strong for so many people, and I am used to concealing emotions (bad or good) that I do not want to share. I found that I had to give my powerful question the freedom to take me to the places I needed to be, to have the conversations I needed to have, and to experience and feel whatever was necessary in the moment. For me it was and still is difficult to take hold of the freedom to just BE, the freedom to allow the peace I know to be the peace I live. But my journey is not finished.

My life has not changed much, nor have the people in my life; rather it is I who have changed because of my powerful question. My life has always been one of service, helping, listening, supporting, and giving peace. I say these things not for accolades or pity, just as facts. I enjoy giving to others. Making others happy makes me happy. My only criticism is that it is very draining, and without proper tools to heal and rejuvenate, one can become emotionally, physically, and spiritually exhausted.

There have been times when I have been completely depleted, and while to the outside world I was fine, internally I was in the desert without a water source. Going through the powerful question process helped me realize that I don't have to serve till it hurts. I coined my previous way of life the "Martha Syndrome."

The story of Martha and Mary always perplexed me, and I took issue with Mary sitting at the feet of Jesus enjoying all that comes with that moment and poor Martha running around taking care of everyone and everything. I so identified with Martha that I was actually upset with the way Jesus spoke to her. I really did not like hearing this Gospel proclaimed.

Do I still struggle with the Martha Syndrome? Yes, sometimes, but now my powerful question helps me recognize it. I am more present to what is happening in the moment—not just present with whomever I am serving but present with an awareness of self as well. God wants us to serve and love one another, but God also wants us to be aware of our own needs, so we can continue to serve.

I intentionally take small yet significant moments to experience peace in my daily life. Instead of going to work and going straight to the office, I stop and go through the church. Stopping at the tabernacle, I let out a breath of air and say, "Good morning, Jesus," followed by prayer and intentions. I do not have the words to tell you what it feels like to begin my day that way, but it is the peace I know.

Throughout the day, I allow myself moments when I just breathe and BE. This is time to inhale and exhale, peace.

Before I go home each day, I go back into the church and stop at the tabernacle. I say, "Good night, Jesus; thank you for my day." I pray and then go home.

This peace I know, but do not always live, has no words that could fully explain or do justice to it. I felt it before, and there is nothing like it, "the peace . . . that surpasses all understanding" (Philippians 4:7). It does not feel deserved, but I know it is from God. I no longer have to feel guilty about taking care of myself.

Before I began this journey to my powerful question, I could not imagine its impact. Now I cannot imagine my life without it. I continue to pray for all those just beginning the journey, that they might experience the transformation I have.

When I first met Shanedra, she was working for a corporation in a role she found stifling. She is now directing one of the most caring homeless outreach efforts in Milwaukee.

How many more Shanedras would it take to change the world? How many more powerful questions?

Oliver Wendell Holmes wrote, "A man may fulfill the object of his existence by asking a question he cannot answer, and attempting a task he cannot achieve."[24] Those are bold words, but what do they mean?

Albert Einstein spent the final twenty-five years of his life trying to discover a unified field theory, a theory that would tie all matter and energy in existence into one theory. Such a theory—sometimes called the Theory of Everything—would explain the cosmos as well as the smallest atomic particle. Einstein endured insults and derision from colleagues who felt he had lost touch with reality. Having achieved all the acclaim anyone could want, trying to solve this mystery was more important than how others viewed him. Today scientists know that he was on to something.

The Light Gets In, and It May Be Blinding

Initially I thought a powerful question was a way to achieve the kind of success people like Steve Jobs enjoyed. But I was only seeing the externals, the outward signs of achievement. I didn't yet understand the internal changes that accompany a most powerful question—the kind of transformations that Shanedra described. These are truly the most important achievements of all.

As we pursue our powerful question, we unpack our tightly held narratives and reconfigure ourselves. This unpacking often occurs with unexpected jolts, and the finished product is not always recognizable until the process is complete. Each stage contains challenges and opportunities we can choose to act on or not. How far we travel and how much transformation occurs depends on our desire to live a purposeful life and our commitment to the process.

The initial period following the discovery of one's powerful question is often a period of not knowing what to make of it. The narrative we have created over a lifetime, in an attempt to understand our life, might now feel inadequate, inaccurate, or very unsettled. For some, this period involves no more than a gentle shift, but for others it can be jarring, like a piece of granite cracking open. Many need time to process this new awareness before they start any sort of search for an answer.

How we search for an answer to our question will likely reflect our personality and openness to change. We can rush right out and search for an answer, as I did, or we can spend time considering this newfound discovery. A teacher might do research, a musician might explore an answer through music, a dancer might choose . . . you get the idea.

There is no time limit. It took me seven years to come up with a workable definition of "boundary." I travelled down numerous side trips in my discovery process, each one providing new insights and possibilities.

During this initial period, we are likely to become aware of things we never noticed before or reconsider things we previously dismissed as irrelevant. I became intensely interested in art and poetry, areas I had little use for previously. Mark Rothko's abstract art was especially meaningful, with its various fields of rectangular color. Those fields of color created boundary events that drew me into new levels of awareness.

The only "must do" during this initial period is to stay attuned to your most powerful question and where it is leading you. Remember Dr. Moustakas's words: "I just follow my question every day." His message was that pursuing a powerful question is more important than finding the answer. Staying with the question creates the tension necessary for God's truth to emerge.

New Glasses

As we grow accustomed to living with our powerful question and begin to develop some understanding of its significance, we start to experience a new level of intuitiveness. We might have moments of serendipitous discovery and encounter what seem like strange coincidences. In short, we start to see new connections through the lens of our powerful question.

Breakthroughs and unexpected answers to problems at work or in our personal life will come. An engineer trying to design a new space capsule, for example, might see the design emerging from within her question. A manager trying to motivate employees at a car dealership might find an approach as he works from the perspective of his question. Over time our powerful question incorporates every aspect of our life, because it taps into what is authentically us. Anything less leaves us unsatisfied.

In the realm of most powerful questions, things happen that we wouldn't have imagined or predicted. Why? Because we now live in a state of meaningful purpose, guided by a deeper level of intuition. We are aware that God has a plan and we have a part to play in it. We let go of expectations and outcomes. We're free to live in truth and listen for God's voice, as we give up trying to control what we cannot or need not control. We move beyond ourselves and into ultimate purpose and meaning.

?

CHAPTER TEN

The Spirituality (and Psychology) of the Most Important Question

Discovering one's most powerful question is a psychological quest and a spiritual one. Meaning and purpose are essential to both quests. To leave out the spiritual aspect of human behavior is to leave out God. To leave out the human aspect of the spiritual is to leave out what God has created in his image and likeness. Powerful questions are a way to bring these aspects of our nature together and enhance our understanding of and appreciation for both.

From its earliest days, psychology was promoted as a healing art, but along the way it took a left-brain turn, seduced by the allure of being scientific. In its early years, psychology focused on diagnosis and various forms of talk therapy. Today medication has largely taken center stage as the treatment of choice. Psychology needs to embrace, not run away from, the spiritual aspect of being human if it is to regain respect as a healing art.

By the same token, the current spiritual trend is overly judgmental and doctrinaire. Lots of energy is spent on determining who possesses the "real" truth, who is "saved" and who is not. This promotes a tribal mentality that makes people feel separate and alienated from each other. These disputes obscure the gospel message that calls us to love our neighbor.

Because I'm a psychologist, people often ask me where this powerful question approach fits in the larger world of human behavior. I'm trained to think of human behavior as a product of both nature (biology) and nurture (environmental influences). As a Catholic, I see God's movement in all matters, big and small. Powerful questions ignite passion; draw a person toward authentic, self-aware living (psychology); and lead them to a purposeful life in union with God's truth (spirituality).

In the early days of my therapeutic practice, I maintained an artificial boundary between the spiritual and the psychological. I'm embarrassed to admit it, but I once advised a counselor that it was wrong to have a Bible on his office bookshelf. Over time I came to realize that my attitude was a barrier to my responding in a genuine, wholistic manner.

The fact is that healing emotional wounds is healing spiritual wounds. These wounds are inseparable.

Spirituality

The word *spiritual* describes the hunger and the longing for God that exists in all of us. A powerful question is a commitment to self-awareness and truth as the catalyst for growth and transformation. When we pursue truth, we pursue God.

My brother Jim, a successful investment advisor, provides a great example in this regard. Five years ago, when I first introduced the concept of powerful questions to him, it didn't take him long to arrive at his. That question came from his deep desire to live a life he could commit to fully. His question, "Why should I believe in Jesus?" spoke to his need to know and not just believe.

Jim was convinced that he needed to answer that question in order to live in line with Jesus' teachings. He took this journey seriously. In addition to prayer and reflection, he read books and spoke with religious leaders. He made two pilgrimages to the Holy Land and ventured into regions considered less than safe.

Five years later, Jim is certain in his heart, mind, and soul that Jesus is God. Before this journey, he "felt" there was a God, but he didn't know it as he does now. His journey and his question have evolved as he strives to know how to live each day as if it is his last.

I'm struck by Jim's journey and his sincere search for truth he could live by. I wonder how many of us have actually asked ourselves if God is real. If we believe it, really believe it, what changes do we have to make in our daily life?

Pope Benedict XVI alludes to this in his book *Jesus of Nazareth*. "It goes without saying that this book is in no way an exercise of the magisterium, but is solely an expression of my personal search 'for the face of the Lord' (cf. Ps 27:8)."[25]

Powerful questions allow us not only to reflect on God's message but also to integrate that message into our life in a deep way. This is very much in line with the Ignatian tradition of the daily Examen. This spiritual practice is designed to help us look at our experiences (our story) on a daily basis and discover God's movement there. What happened to me today? Were there moments when I felt the divine presence?

Similarly, when we look through the lens of a powerful question, God's movements come into focus. Then we can integrate them into our life experiences.

Both/And

People following their powerful question benefit both psychologically and spiritually, as they become fully alive to who they are and therefore freer to seek God's truth.

Sue is a woman who carries her truth and her cross with saintly dignity. She attended a powerful question retreat and arrived at the following question: "What is the good in suffering?" Her story speaks for itself.

I grew up in poverty. My dad was a pilot. He was injured during a plane crash and ruptured his pancreas and could not work. My mom worked as a legal secretary, though with six kids, that money didn't go far. My only brother suffered three hemorrhages in his thalamus and was brain injured. The last bleed put him in a coma, which affected his short-term memory. During these times when my brother was in intensive care, we would pray the Rosary every night as a family.

Like most poor children, we didn't realize how poor we were. As we grew up and became teenagers, food stamps and living in the projects bothered us. I lied about where I lived. I couldn't bring myself to say, "I live in the housing projects." Human Concerns ministry at our church would bring us food on Thanksgiving and Easter and toys at Christmastime. Because of that support, I grew up having so much admiration for the Catholic Church.

At age sixteen, I was hit by a car while riding my bike. My ankle was crushed, not broken, which meant multiple surgeries. At one time, we had three hospital beds in our living room. I would say, "It looks like Calcutta in here," while my mom chimed in, "You three have mattresses though."

Years passed, and I met a wonderful man who didn't care if he was picking me up from the projects. We married and had two beautiful daughters. I was so grateful to have a working husband who allowed me to be a stay-at-home mom.

As the girls grew up, I worked part-time. I was drawn to working with the elderly, the sick, and the less fortunate. I applied to the archdiocese to take the lay ministry certificate program. Those were some of the happiest four years of my life.

Once out of school, I was able to serve the poor in a variety of ministries without costing a parish any money. We made diapers from recycled T-shirts, sanitary pads for women, burial gowns from recycled wedding dresses, prayer shawls from donated yarn. I worked at the parish for sixteen years, and serving those experiencing extreme poverty was the bulk of my work.

I was diagnosed with Parkinson's disease in June of 2014. I was grieving the loss of my capabilities when, in September of 2018, I lost my twenty-five-year-old daughter to an accidental drug overdose. One month later I had surgery to have a deep brain stimulator inserted in my brain. In intense grief over the loss of my daughter, I decided to have the surgery because of what I figured was a win-win situation. I would either die on the operating table and get to see Natalie, or I would be able to move better.

The surgery was a success. I was able to resume working part-time, driving, walking, and enjoying my hobbies.

After discovering my powerful question—"What is the good of suffering?"—I began a bereavement ministry at my parish, including a grief support group. I now work with Human Concerns to build affordable housing in Milwaukee, and I teach grade schoolers how to make mattresses using crocheted plastic bags.

In opening to my own suffering from life losses, I enhance my desire to be of service to those around me. I become truly available at a deeper level of my soul. I do not deny pain, but I open myself to what it is trying to teach me.

When Sue first told me what her question was, I took a deep breath and braced myself for what was surely going to be a depressing story. Instead she helped me understand the words of St. Irenaeus: "The glory of God is man fully alive." Sue inspires others to glorify God and redefines what it means to be fully alive through suffering.

Sue's story also reminds me of Pope St. John Paul II, who lived his final years in suffering, visible to the whole world. Some think he should have quietly stepped down, but he showed us the grace in living fully alive, even in the midst of suffering.

?

CHAPTER ELEVEN

The Powerful Question, the Church, and Beyond

Growing in faith involves growing in knowledge of, connection to, and love for God. Children process the concept of faith by watching and imitating how their parents and others practice it in their daily life. Adult growth involves moving beyond rules and rituals to a more personal relationship with Jesus Christ. We cannot achieve growth in faith by ourselves; we need a real relationship with Jesus Christ, not just an image of him we hang on a wall.

The path we travel to our place in God's plan may have detours and potholes, but it also has a refueling station, our local parish. At a basic level, a parish has a building, the church, in which we house the tabernacle and engage in the sacraments. But a parish is more than that: it's a community of people sharing their faith journey and drawing others into that journey and community.

As a community, however, the parish only works if we are active members and not just bystanders. What happens when family gatherings occur and only a few show up? What happens when people arrive at family gatherings and just sit in a corner by themselves?

Any family, any real community, will experience the tension that creates togetherness and that at times tests relationships. That came to the forefront during the recent pandemic, when we had a virtual parish experience and learned we could carry on. Our shared history and parish belongingness enabled that to happen.

The Challenge

Will it be enough to tell God on judgment day, "I loved my parents, I loved my family and friends, I loved my children"? I expect God might answer, "So, who wouldn't?" No, I think we'll have to answer for those we have welcomed or failed to welcome in our life, directly and indirectly, not just family and friends. Our parish is the natural starting place to experience the kind of community that lets us love our neighbors.

Increasingly the Catholic Church in the United States relies on lay ministers to keep parishes running. It goes without saying that lay ministers are intricately linked to the future and the hope of the Church. Where do these ministers come from? They come from the front, middle, and back pews of parishes. They step forward to help when ministries are in need. But typically they represent a small fraction of the congregation.

Why is this? Some people fail to volunteer because they feel they have little to offer; others blame cliques that form in certain parish ministries; still others mention priests who will not share responsibilities. The ever-ready excuse is that other demands on time and energy leave nothing for parish ministry or service.

This situation will only change when we recognize that being Catholic means being involved as an active member of a parish. The backbone of the Catholic Church is the parish community, with lay ministers serving as the hands and legs. With the current shortage of priests, lay ministers shoulder more and more of the administration and evangelization duties in parish communities. Administration is important, and evangelization is critical. History and logic teach us that any parish community not growing is likely declining.

The Evangelizing Mission

Evangelization means taking God's message into the world, inviting others—by example and word—to experience the gifts and graces that await them in the Catholic Church. We generally don't go places unless we feel invited. For the average person, telling them what they "should" do is not an effective or enticing invitation. Working within the context of a powerful question is a more intuitive and relational approach to evangelization.

Rhonda is one of the most effective and dedicated evangelizers I have ever had the privilege of knowing. As I met parishioners in Milwaukee, I often asked them how they became involved at a deeper level with their faith. I stopped asking this question in one area of town, because it seemed the answer was always "Because of Rhonda." Rhonda ran women's support groups in her parish. She completed a program to be certified as a spiritual director.

Rhonda agreed to share her thoughts about her powerful question and its connection with evangelization:

To me nothing is more important than one's intimate, loving, personal relationship with Jesus. I did what I could to invite, encourage, and help others encounter or experience Jesus. It was frustrating when my attempts did not seem to work.

In our secular society, for increasing numbers of people, God is not even on their radar. How then will they fall in love with Jesus? Love certainly isn't something that can be forced. Furthermore, is it even realistic to expect everyone to have an encounter with the Lord leading to a conversion of heart? Maybe not. What then?

Jesus must be more than just a blip on someone's radar screen and more than a passing interest. I desire that people become absorbed in, fascinated with, and captivated by Jesus and compelled to know him more. So my powerful question is "How does someone become enthralled with Jesus?"

It is my belief that enthrallment will ultimately lead to conversion of heart and an intimate relationship with Jesus. I see enthrallment as the necessary state one must enter to be "found" by Jesus. Jesus is seeking a relationship with us. Are we seeking one with him?

The process of my powerful question revealing itself to me required a significant amount of worthwhile soul searching. It has given resolution to a restless feeling from within that I could not quite name. For some people, the search for an answer will be a driving force. It was for me too, until a satisfying answer came to me. It is the living out of the answer that has now provided clarity and direction.

Someone becomes enthralled with Jesus through the authentic witness of others. I am called to be that authentic witness.

My powerful question is an evangelization tool, because it energizes and enlivens me to go forth and spread the good news of the gospel and invite others to join me. Second, it enables each person's experience of or encounter with God to be distinctly individual and uniquely theirs. I keep inviting others to varied opportunities, not knowing which one will be "it" for that person. Since the process of articulating one's powerful question gets to the heart of what one cares about most deeply or what one most desires, it necessarily leads to contemplation of God and response to him.

These powerful questions often produce actions to serve, help, or improve. Cultivating a servant's heart is an inroad to discipleship. Incorporating one's charisms into one's powerful question can help one discern what God's will is for them, their purpose. The living out of their powerful question will give meaning to *their life: John 10:10: "I came so that they might have life and have it more abundantly."*

Inviting someone to find their powerful question may lead them to an encounter with Jesus and a life lived to the full. In a nutshell, a powerful question can initiate or enrich one's relationship with God.

Asking a person if they have a powerful question invites them to share what they want on a deeper level. This is the same invitation that Jesus offered Andrew when he stopped and asked him and another disciple of John the Baptist what they wanted (see John 1:35-40). A sincere inquiry of this type lets people know we care about them as unique individuals. Those who respond are looking for a deeper relationship with Jesus Christ, whether they express it that way or not.

As a person becomes more curious and starts to think about finding their own question, we share how that question has deepened our relationship with Jesus Christ and led us to our role in his mission. The key here is to trust that anyone who pursues truth about themselves will also encounter God. This encounter will be something they trust, because it originates within themselves.

Lay ministers can use their own powerful questions to energize evangelization efforts parish-wide. They can introduce the concept and set up classes for those who want to find their most powerful question. This can be within adult spiritual growth classes or some other format. The ways in which powerful questions dovetail with and deepen faith will be evident in those who attend. In the appendix to this book, I've suggested guidelines for parish leaders who, having found their own powerful question, want to help others do the same.

The bottom line is that parish involvement is crucial for those who want to grow in faith. It follows that finding a most powerful question has the potential not only to increase parish involvement and service but also, and most importantly, to help parishioners grow in faith on an ever-deepening level. The parish is where faith and contemplation meet and lead to action.

And Beyond

What kind of action might faith and contemplation lead to?

As more parishioners find their most powerful question and intensify their commitment to their parish, consider how that new life could manifest itself, even beyond the parish. Consider, for example, what might happen if high school students had the opportunity to find a powerful question. After I presented powerful question classes to students in one Catholic high school, the principal, Mrs. Maria Modelski, wrote:

The powerful question approach to discernment was a tremendous complement to our curriculum. Dr. John could accomplish more in one hour of working with our students than we could in a week! He helped them think and reflect, to identify themes in their lives and areas of strength and weakness. He encouraged them to look inward and see what drove them: to ask questions, to constantly search for truth, to see what thoughts were recurring and what they could never solve but were always curious about.

By exploring these questions, students were able to move toward identifying their own powerful question—something that would stay with them for the rest of their lives as they continued to move forward and seek God's will. In many ways, this was the most important part of our curriculum. Our lives are a process of discovery, and by prayerfully considering what God is calling them to be at such a formative time in their lives, our students were more prepared to consider their vocation and to live it more fully.

Would the most powerful question approach make a difference if applied to "real world" problems? Putting on my psychologist hat, I recognize several groups of people who could benefit enormously if they were encouraged to find their powerful question.

The first are those caught in what we euphemistically refer to as a midlife crisis. These are men and women, typically between the ages of forty and sixty, who feel rudderless and dissatisfied with the life they spent so much time and effort creating. They wonder, Is that all there is?

The answer, of course, is no. And seeking an answer through golf, gardening, or sports cars works only briefly—and never long enough to make a lasting improvement in mood. Finding a powerful question works much better, because it ignites passion and reveals purpose over the long term.

Another group who would benefit from this approach is harder to reach: young people caught in the deadly spiral of gangs, drugs, and violence. The first step in reclaiming these young lives involves motivating and empowering them to ask discerning questions about life and their life in particular. If a young person can ask those kinds of questions, they can start to see themselves as a person, one who has a place in the world and in God's plan.

Young people in gangs or using drugs typically function like a bundle of loosely held-together cells that float fairly aimlessly, unable to act but only to react to whatever blunt force they encounter. And as we know, many of these young people have had plenty of blunt force in their lives: trauma and dashed hopes. They may be able to breathe in but not out.

Motivating vulnerable young people to ask reflective, discerning questions about their life is likely to lead to further awareness and, with God's help, to their powerful question. That will enable them to feel hope and purpose beating in their hearts.

We saw this play out in Laura MacDonald's work with youth in her mountain-bike program. She sees every one of these young people through the lens of her question, "What is legacy?" (see chapter 2, "Discovering My Question").

In the long run, motivating vulnerable youth to ask discerning questions—motivating anyone to do so, in fact—is most likely to occur through the efforts of those who see through the lens of their own most powerful question. I firmly believe that as more people find their most powerful question, we will begin to see new ways of breathing life and purpose into the Church and beyond, to those who need it the most. As a Catholic and as a Christian, I believe that a person who finds purpose finds God.

Acknowledgments

First and foremost, thanks to my wife, Margaret, who suffered through endless rewrites and the ups and downs that accompanied them.

Tonja Acker-Richards, Roslyn McGrath, Patty O'Neal, Dr. Karen Duquette, Caryn Schutte, Barbara McBride-Schmitt, Norma Semashko, Ruth Almen, Carole Pence, Ralph Kanaar, David Cowell, Michele Bentti, Louise Reichert, Jenni Bartholomew, Ann Owen, Bonnie Shafrin, Brandon Bruckman, and Laurie Hammar for their editing help, encouragement, and support.

The brave individuals who took a chance on My Powerful Question in its formation stages, especially Christi Pentecost and Nancy Caldwell, who sponsored the first class through their entrepreneurial support organization; Maria Modelski, former principal of St. Michael the Archangel High School, who introduced Powerful Question to her students as a pilot program; Dr. Patrick Russell, Julie O'Connor, Jenny Drzewiecki, and all the staff and faculty of Sacred Heart Seminary and School of Theology in Milwaukee, who helped bring Powerful Question to life in their graduate program of studies.

Jon Sweeney for his editing help. Monica Misey for her tireless work to promote the Powerful Question vision. Joe Durepos, my agent, for his expertise and guidance in finding the right publisher. Beth McNamara, for being the right publisher and the person who found a home for this book at The Word Among Us Press.

And finally, the Board of Directors of the Powerful Question Institute—Joe Hilke, Sally Smits, Monica Misey, Cindy Rusnak, Michelle Nemer, Edell Schaefer, Sharon Hanson, Terri Engsberg, Diane Scott, and Margaret Olesnavage—for their faithful support and guidance.

?

Guidelines for Helping People Find Their Question

As people go through the discernment process described in this book and experience its transforming effects, they feel a natural desire to help others find their most powerful question. We want to encourage that but also protect the integrity of this approach to finding purpose, growing in love for God, and moving toward discipleship. To that end, I've developed guidelines for those helping others find their most important question.

First and foremost, recognize that this is a self-directed discernment process. The focus is on what a person discovers for themselves in their life review and reflection. The question that emerges may not meet someone else's perceptions or expectations.

Second, this is not spiritual counseling, mental health counseling, coaching, or any other form of "treatment." It is not giving advice. Persons providing encouragement, support, and feedback need to leave their other hats at the door and be willing to simply be present to those discerning their question. Being present means listening to what the other shares and respecting that person's process. Their powerful question is theirs to discover. It is not up to a support person to determine whether it is the right one or not. Attempting to direct a person to a particular conclusion will diminish the discovery process and hinder any real discernment.

Along those same lines, please use the steps offered in this book (see chapter 8). They have proven effective with hundreds of people in numerous settings. You might want to invent new steps or strategies, and they might even appear beneficial. But they might also cross boundaries, such as those referenced above.

Third, it's not helpful to try to figure out or analyze the discerner's emotional or psychological needs. It is appropriate to offer feedback, but the most useful feedback often involves asking a person what they mean by certain words or phrases.

When a person shares painful memories, feedback might include a compassionate or empathetic "I'm so sorry for what you've been through" or "That must have been very painful." A person's responses to such comments shouldn't be challenged. However, it can be fine to ask for clarification, in a nonjudgmental tone, when those answers seem disconnected or defensive.

If a person demonstrates an obvious need for additional help, it may be appropriate to ask if they have considered seeking professional support. Keep in mind, however, that asking about mental health history, medications, and similar details is inappropriate, can lead to advice giving, and will likely hinder the discernment process. Depending on circumstances, it may be appropriate to remind the person that this process requires some clear emotional space in which to work. People in crisis are usually not able to engage in thoughtful reflection.

Fourth, when the person has established timelines, identified important themes, and reflected on them, the next step is helping them name what they do not know about those themes. Remind them that the most powerful question is going to be the one to which they don't know the answer. You can help by asking clarifying questions, but don't give your own opinions or compare their journey to your journey or anyone else's. At this stage, you might want to suggest that they pray and ask God to reveal the question he wants them to discover.

Assure the person that when the most powerful question arrives, it will be accompanied by a physical or emotional response. This will vary from individual to individual, and so your only job is to ask them if they feel they received the kind of response that tells them this is the right question. Here again, they are the final authority on whether the physical or emotional response was sufficient affirmation. If they say yes, your job as a helper is over, except to congratulate them and ask if they know how they might want to pursue an answer.

Assure them that they can sit with their question for a while. It takes time to absorb what has happened, what they might have recognized for the first time in their life. And if it's appropriate, you can always suggest that they join with others who are pursuing their own most powerful question through the Powerful Question Institute. You'll find contact information in the Resources section that follows.

God bless you in your efforts. You are serving others and serving God.

Notes

1. Rachel Carson, *Silent Spring* (New York: Houghton Mifflin Harcourt, 1962).
2. Quote from plaque honoring St. Vincent de Paul in the DePaul University Library, Chicago, Illinois: "He followed this question into sainthood."
3. Quoted in Walter Isaacson, *Einstein: His life and Universe* (New York: Simon and Schuster, 2007), 114.
4. Isaacson, *Steve Jobs* (New York: Simon and Schuster, 2011), 61.
5. Brian Kolodiejchuk, ed., *Mother Teresa: Come Be My Light* (New York: Doubleday, 2007).
6. Maya Lin, *Boundaries* (New York: Simon and Schuster, 2000), 3:05.
7. See Daniel H. Pink, *Drive: The Surprising Truth about What Motivates Us* (New York: Riverhead, 2009).

8. "Sojourner Truth, 1797–1883," www. Sojournertruth.com.

9. Ibid.

10. Lin, 3:09.

11. Chris Baker, "The Creator, an Interview with Will," *Wired* Magazine, August 2012, 66–70.

12. A. H. Maslow, *Motivation and Personality* (New York: Harper and Row, 1954).

13. Andrew Hodges, *Alan Turing*: The Enigma (Princeton, NJ: Princeton University Press, 2014).

14. Richard Bach, *Running from Safety: An Adventure of the Spirit* (New York: Delta, 1994), 112.

15. Amy Woodyatt, "49 Journalists were murdered in 2019, the lowest death toll in 16 years," *CNN Business*, December 17, 2019, https://www.cnn.com/2019/12/17/media/rsf-journalists-killed-intl-scli/index.html.

16. Elizabeth Bettina, *It Happened in Italy: Untold Stories of How the People of Italy Defied the Horrors of the Holocaust* (Nashville, TN: Thomas Nelson, 2009), 12.

17. Viktor E. Frankl, *Man's Search for Meaning (Boston, MA: Beacon Press, 1959).*

18. Jill W. Iscol and Peter W. Cookson, *Hearts on Fire: Stories of Today's Visionaries Igniting Idealism into Action* (New York: Random House, 2012), 138.

19. see Paul W. King, *Climbing Maslow's Pyramid* (Leics, UK: Troubador Publishing, 2009).

20. Rev. Martin Luther King, "I've Been to the Mountaintop," April 3, 1968, https://www.americanrhetoric.com/speeches/mlkivebeentothemountaintop.htm.

21. Abraham Maslow, *The Farther Reaches of Human Nature* (New York: Viking, 1971).

22. Frankl, 175.

23. Thomas Merton, *No Man Is an Island* (San Diego, CA: Harcourt, 2005), 246.

24. Oliver Wendell Holmes, as quoted in Grenville Kleiser, *Dictionary of Proverbs* (New Delhi: A.P.H. Publishing, 2005), 8.

25. Pope Benedict XVI, *Jesus of Nazareth: From the Baptism in the Jordan to the Transfiguration* (San Francisco: Ignatius, 2007), xxiii.

Bibliography

Adams, Douglas. *The Hitchhiker's Guide to the Galaxy.* New York: Del Rey, reissue ed., 1995.

American Psychiatric Association. *Desk Reference to the Diagnostic Criteria from DSM-5.* Arlington, VA: American Psychiatric Association, 2013.

Atwood, Margaret. *The Year of the Flood.* New York: Doubleday, 2009.

Baker, Chris. "The Creator, an Interview with Will." *Wired* Magazine, August 2012, 66–70.

Barry, John M. *The Great Influenza: The Story of the Deadliest Pandemic in History.* New York: Penguin, 2005.

Bettina, Elizabeth. *It Happened in Italy: Untold Stories of How the People of Italy Defied the Horrors of the Holocaust.* Nashville, TN: Thomas Nelson, 2009.

Bordon, Sarah. *Edith Stein.* New York: Continuum, 2003.

Borghesi, Massimo. *The Mind of Pope Francis: Jorge Mario Bergoglio's Intellectual Journey*. Collegeville, MN: Liturgical Press, 2018.

Buckley, Michael, J. *What Do You Seek? The Questions of Jesus as Challenge and Promise*. Grand Rapids, MI: Eerdmans, 2016.

Dowling, William C. *Ricoeur on Time and Narrative: An Introduction to Temps et Récit*. Notre Dame, IN: University of Notre Dame Press, 2011.

Fanon, Frantz. *The Wretched of the Earth*. Translated by Richard Philcox. New York: Grove, 2004.

Frankl, Viktor. *Man's Search for Meaning*. Boston: Beacon Press, 1959.

Isaacson, Walter: *Einstein: His Life and Universe*. New York: Simon and Schuster, 2007.

Keller, Gary, with Jay Papasan. *The One Thing: The Surprisingly Simple Truth Behind Extraordinary Results*. Austin, TX: Bard Press, 2012.

Linkner, Josh. *Disciplined Dreaming: A Proven System to Drive Breakthrough Creativity*. San Francisco, CA: Jossey-Bass, 2011.

McAdams, Dan P. *The Stories We Live By: Personal Myths and the Making of the Self*. New York: Guilford Press, 1993.

McDougall, Christopher. *Born to Run: A Hidden Tribe, Superathletes, and the Greatest Race the World Has Never Seen*. New York: Knof/Doubleday, 2011.

Merton, Thomas. *Thoughts in Solitude*. New York: Farrar, Straus and Cudahy, 1959.

Moore, Michael. *Here Comes Trouble: Stories from My Life*. New York: Hatchette Book Group, 2011.

Moore, Michael. *Roger & Me*. 1989 documentary film.

Moore, Pete. *E=mc²: The Great Ideas That Shaped Our World*. New York: Metro Books, 2002.

Moustakas, Clark E. *Existential Psychotherapy and the Interpretation of Dreams*. New York: Jason Aronson, 1994.

Pink, Daniel H. *Drive: The Surprising Truth about What Motivates Us*. New York: Riverhead, 2009.

Ratzinger, Joseph, Pope Benedict XVI. *Jesus of Nazareth: From the Baptism in the Jordan to the Transfiguration*. New York: Doubleday, 2007.

Reber, Arthur S. *Penguin Dictionary of Psychology*. New York: Penguin, 2nd ed., 1995.

Russell, Patrick, J. *The God Questions: What Forms and Shapes Us*. Liguori, MO: Liguori Publications, 2007.

Senior, Donald et al, eds. *The Catholic Study Bible*. New York: Oxford University Press, 1990.

Dr. Seuss. *Oh, The Places You'll Go!* New York: Random House, 1990.

Shotter, J. "At the Boundaries of Being: Re-figuring Intellectual Life." Paper presented at UNH Conference, Social Construction and Relational Practices, September, 1999.

Sobel, Andrew, and Jerold Panas. *Power Questions: Build Relationships, Win New Business, and Influence Others*. Hoboken, NJ: Wiley and Sons, 2012.

Stein, Edith. *On the Problem of Empathy.* Translated by
Waltraut Stein. Washington: ICS Publications, 1989.

Strecher, Victor, J. *Life On Purpose: How Living for
What Matters Most Changes Everything.* New York:
Harper Collins, 2016.

U.S. News and World Report, Interview with Elie Wiesel,
October 27, 1986.

Vance, Ashlee. *Elon Musk: Tesla, SpaceX, and the Quest
for a Fantastic Future.* New York: Ecco, 2015.

Winnicott, D.W. *Winnicott on the Child.* Cambridge,
MA: Da Capo Press, 2002.

?

The Powerful Question Institute

- The Powerful Question Institute is a nonprofit whose purpose is "to promote Powerful Questions as a way to enhance personal growth and heal a fractured world." See www.askyourpowerfulquestion.com.

- We have a Facebook group: "Powerful Question Institute."

- An annual conference aimed at exploring new avenues of development, celebrating accomplishments, and reestablishing connections is in the planning stages.

- Dr. Olesnavage is available for retreats and workshops. He can be contacted at johnolesnavage@gmail.com.